The Greens in British Politics

James Dennison

The Greens in British Politics

Protest, Anti-Austerity and the Divided Left

palgrave
macmillan

James Dennison
European University Institute
San Domenico di Fiesole FI, Italy

ISBN 978-3-319-42672-3 ISBN 978-3-319-42673-0 (eBook)
DOI 10.1007/978-3-319-42673-0

Library of Congress Control Number: 2016957871

Printed on acid-free paper

This Palgrave Macmillan imprint is published by Springer Nature
The registered company is Springer International Publishing AG
The registered company address is: Gewerbestrasse 11, 6330 Cham, Switzerland

Acknowledgements

There are a number of people whom I would like to thank for helping to make this project a reality. Two colleagues, without whom the project would have been far more difficult, deserve special acknowledgement. Hanspeter Kriesi was a consistent source of guidance, wisdom and, as importantly, morale throughout the process and beyond. Matthew Goodwin's energy, ideas and willingness to discuss challenges and opportunities, in numerous ways, made writing this book a far more exciting process. Kalypso Nicolaïdis and Geoff Evans gave me the timely opportunity to work at Nuffield College during the last election, every day of which was, not least because of their involvement, inspiring and fulfilling. Working with Sarah Birch offered direction in writing, while comparing notes on the Greens was a real pleasure. Harold Clarke's encouragement and insights gave me additional confidence in this study. Hearing Lynn Bennie's expertise on the Scottish Greens was useful and added perspective to the study. Tim Bale, Paul Webb and, particularly, Monica Poletti went out of their way to share data from their Party Members Project on the Green Party's membership, which was key to reinforcing the empirical findings of the book. Finally, I would like to thank Alistair McMillan and Simon Hix for their consistent support and enthusiasm.

I also must thank the Green Party's members, candidates and staff who were extremely open, frank and engaging in the interviews that fed into many of this study's findings. Our conversations, some of which went on for hours and could have quite easily gone on longer, were vastly informative, and the passion and belief that they have in their cause are inspiring. All went out of their way to help us both make sense of what has happened to their party over the last few years. Regardless of one's political persuasion, I have no doubt that every Green with whom I spoke was involved in politics for the right reasons, often making great sacrifices in the process.

Finally, and most importantly, Eirini's love, understanding and patience helped me through every stage of writing this book from beginning to end.

Contents

1	The Rise of the Greens in British Politics	1
2	Usual Low in an Increasingly Favourable Context	11
3	'Green Spike': European Elections to Independence Referendum	35
4	'Green Surge': Becoming England's Third Largest Party	63
5	Car Crashes, Campaigning and Partial Decline	83
6	Who Voted Green and Why?	107
7	Explaining Constituency-Level Green Success	123
8	Conclusion: Protest, Anti-Austerity and the Divided Left	135
Bibliography		147
Index		149

List of Figures

Fig. 1.1	The polling and membership of the Green Party of England and Wales, 2012–2015 (Source: ukpollingreport.co.uk, www.greenparty.org.uk)	4
Fig. 1.2	Press coverage and public interest in the GPEW and Natalie Bennett (Source: LexisNexis; Google Trends)	5
Fig. 1.3	The polling and membership of the Scottish Greens, 2014–2015 (Source: www.electoralcalculus.co.uk, British Election Study, www.scottishgreens.org.uk)	6
Fig. 2.1	GPEW and Scottish Green recent electoral history in proportional elections (left) and majoritarian elections (right) (Note: European Parliament vote share combines votes for the GPEW and the Scottish Greens; Welsh Assembly and Scottish Parliament vote share considers only the Regional and not Constituency vote share)	13
Fig. 2.2	Party positions on overall economic and social matters (left) and on the specific issues of tax and spending and immigration (right) (Source: Chapel Hill Experts Survey 1999–2014 Trend File)	23
Fig. 3.1	Polling for the 2014 European Parliament elections and, for the Green Party, the 2009 European Election (The dates of the 2009 European elections are realigned to coincide with the days prior to the election in 2014) (Source: UK Polling Report)	39
Fig. 3.2	Green Party polling for the 2005, 2010 and 2015 General Elections (Source: UK Polling Report)	41
Fig. 3.3	Profile of pro-independence Scottish Green and SNP supporters, October 2014 (Source: British Election Study)	54

Fig. 3.4	Determinants of support for Scottish Greens rather than SNP among pro-independence voters (Source: British Election Study, October 2014)	56
Fig. 3.5	Estimated effects on supporting the Greens rather than the SNP amongst pro-independence voters (Source: British Election Study, October 2014)	57
Fig. 4.1	Profiles of Green Party of England and Wales members by cohort and electorate profile (Source: Party Members Project; British Election Study 2014–2017)	70
Fig.4.2	Past voting record of Green Party of England and Wales members by cohort (Source: Party Members Project; note: figures represent only those eligible to vote at the time)	75
Fig. 4.3	GPEW income and expenditure by year (Source: Electoral Commission)	79
Fig. 5.1	Which party leader has had the best and worst campaign? (Source: British Election Study 2015)	91
Fig. 6.1	Socio-demographic and attitudinal profiles by 2015 party choice	111
Fig. 6.2	Determinants of voting Green in the 2015 UK General Election	114
Fig. 6.3	Marginal effects of statistically significant predictors of voting Green	115
Fig. 6.4	Determinants of voting Green (of (1) 2010 Liberal Democrat voters and (2) those who had intended to vote Labour in early 2014)	117
Fig. 6.5	Fixed effects logistic panel models of leader affinity, party competence and party contact effects	119
Fig. 7.1	Determinants of GPEW constituency vote share	123
Fig. 7.2	Marginal effects of determinants of 2015 GPEW vote share	127
Fig. 7.3	The GPEW's fifteen 'best' and 'worst' performing constituencies	128

CHAPTER 1

The Rise of the Greens in British Politics

Abstract In this chapter, I show how both the Green Party of England and Wales and the Scottish Greens underwent increases in their poll ratings, memberships and national prominence in the year and a half prior to the 2015 General Election. This growth, in England and Wales at least, was proportionately more dramatic than that of any other party and culminated in an unprecedented Green vote share at the General Election as well as the Green Party becoming the third largest party in England and Wales by membership. Moreover, the Greens, at least temporarily, secured a position in the second tier of Britain's refigured party system. The rapidity of these changes, their lack of historic precedent and their counter-intuitiveness make the rise of the Greens in Britain particularly interesting. I go on to outline the structure of this study, as well as the approaches, data and methods that it uses.

Keywords Green Party • General election • Party membership • Political engagement • Protest • Austerity

Britain's Green parties have undergone a comparatively and historically exceptional period of growth since 2014. The three entirely separate and independent parties–the Green Party of England and Wales (GPEW), the Scottish Greens and the Green Party in Northern Ireland–all recorded rapid increases in their memberships and considerably higher vote shares

J. Dennison, *The Greens in British Politics*,
DOI 10.1007/978-3-319-42673-0_1

in elections at all levels from 2014 onwards. Albeit to varying extents, these three parties are now considerably more established in their party systems than they were just a few years earlier. Given the previous secular decline in party memberships across advanced democracies, a contemporary political context that was, arguably, unfavourable to the Greens and the parties' comparatively weak historic electoral performances, understanding the growth of the Greens is vital if we wish to explain on-going changes to politics in Britain and in advanced democracies generally, as well as to the Green political movement worldwide.

This study seeks to explain the growth of the Greens by asking a number of related research questions. What were the effects of changes in the British party system and the political context on the Greens' fortunes? How did the Greens themselves change–ideologically and organisationally–and with what consequences? How did the public and voters respond to these transformations and why? To whom did the Greens appeal? What held the parties back? What does the growth of the Greens tell us about broader changes to democratic politics? For the purposes of this study, the two Green parties in Great Britain–the GPEW and the Scottish Greens–are analysed, owing both to the high growth that they underwent and the prominent positions that they now hold; though the Green Party in Northern Ireland are also considered intermittently. To answer these questions, this study includes extensive quantitative analyses of voters and party members and qualitative findings from interviews with leading party insiders and candidates.

Ultimately, I show that the Greens were able to appeal to a distinct section of the electorate who tended to be young, university educated professionals with relatively low incomes who rented their homes. Politically, these voters were no more left wing than Labour voters but, instead, were particularly dissatisfied with British democracy, had no qualms about voting for a small party and rallied around the banner of anti-austerity. The Greens, whose on-going 'professionalisation' and electoral-focus accelerated in the years after the 2010 General Election, became suddenly relevant to the electorate and media as the only unapologetically anti-austerity party in England and as a left-wing antidote, or even equivalent, to the increasingly prominent populist right. In Scotland, the Greens were able to carve a niche prior to the Scottish Independence Referendum as the party of choice for those who supported independence not as an expression of nationalism but as a route to a fairer society. After the referendum result, party membership became a tool by which pro-independence Scots could express their unwillingness to accept the result of the referendum as final. In England and Wales, an unprecedented 'Green Surge' in membership saw thousands join the party in just a few months as a way to express their dissatisfaction with the Greens' exclusion from the pre-election television debates, despite the populist right's inclusion, and their more fundamental ideological sympathy with the newly visible party. On both sides of the border, the membership surges gave the Greens far greater resources with which to fight their election campaigns. In England and Wales, the Greens, who still retained many of the organisational traits of a minor party, were unable to withstand the scrutiny that their newfound popularity brought, which, combined with the first-past-the-post electoral system, saw the party unable to increase its number of seats, despite a quadrupling of their vote share.

What Rise?

In early 2014 the GPEW consisted of just 14,000 members, a figure that had barely changed since the last election and included many with outstanding membership fees. The party's national political machine was threadbare and largely comprised volunteers outside of its sole Westminster seat, Brighton Pavilion. Moreover, election polls, which had only started to regularly include the Greens in 2012, showed a widespread lack of support for the Greens across Britain; just one per cent of respondents in a December 2013 poll said that they would vote Green at the next general election.[1] The Greens in England and Wales, as well as the entirely independent Scottish Greens, seemed set to maintain their long legacies of paltry vote shares and lost electoral deposits. One party insider commented that the GPEW was "set to do much worse than in 2010" and was "facing wipe-out" at the upcoming European election.

Around April 2014 the Greens' polling figures spiked from two per cent to around five per cent, coinciding with the 2014 European elections and the local elections in England. These two elections saw the GPEW return an additional Member of the European Parliament (MEP), despite a slight decline in vote share, and increase their local election vote share from 3.5 per cent in 2013 to 6.6 per cent, gaining an additional 18 council seats.[2] These modest successes, neither of which were without historic precedent, led the media to increasingly frame the Greens as the 'UKIP of the Left' over the summer of 2014 (Fig. 1.1).

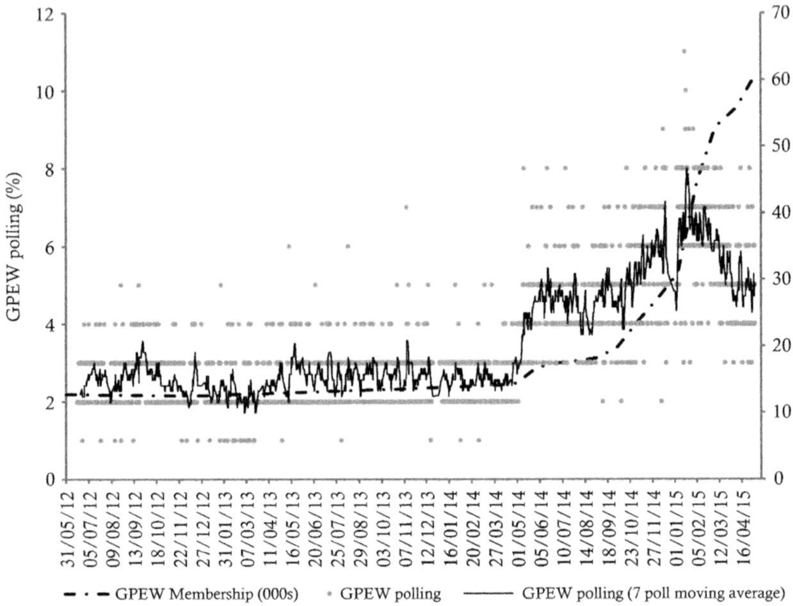

Fig. 1.1 The polling and membership of the Green Party of England and Wales, 2012–2015 (Source: ukpollingreport.co.uk, www.greenparty.org.uk)

A number of events in September triggered a rapid period of growth in the party's polling and membership figures, ushering in what was known at the time as the 'Green Surge'. Above all, the decision by Britain's major television broadcasters to exclude the party from their televised debates sparked an unprecedented rise in the party's membership. In just one week around the New Year, the party recruited 13,000 new members. By February, the party had more members than either UKIP or the Liberal Democrats, making it England's third largest party. Furthermore, the GPEW's polling figures rose from the beginning of October, peaking in late January 2015, when one poll put them at 12 per cent. Simultaneously, the party's profile was boosted in the media, as coverage and public interest in the party and its leader, Natalie Bennett, grew (see Fig. 1.2).

Just as the Greens began to believe they could be on course to make a major breakthrough in the upcoming election, from late January onwards their poll ratings declined rapidly to around five per cent. Their membership continued to rise, albeit at a slower rate, reaching 60,000 by the time

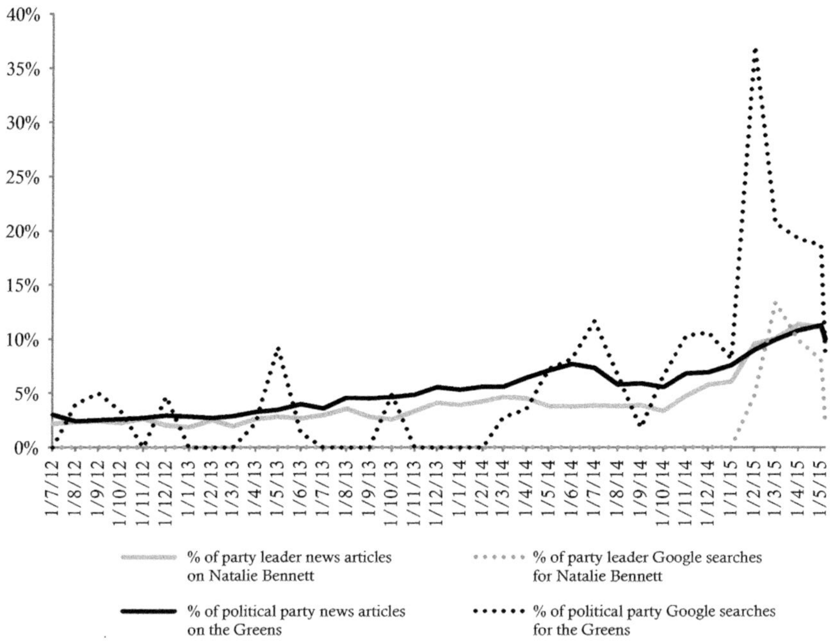

Fig. 1.2 Press coverage and public interest in the GPEW and Natalie Bennett (Source: LexisNexis; Google Trends)

of the election. Additionally, February saw an intense period of public interest in the party, although it was not entirely positive. Ultimately, the 2015 General Election would leave the GPEW with as many seats as they had won in 2010, despite winning four times as many votes.

Meanwhile, the Scottish Greens also underwent their own dramatic membership increase in September 2014 (see Fig. 1.3). Throughout most of 2014, the party membership was stable at around 1,700, while its electoral support grew only slightly. However, in the immediate aftermath of the referendum on Scottish independence, on 18 September, the Scottish Greens underwent a sixfold increase in their membership in just one week. Though this growth in Scotland would not translate into success at the General Election, like in England and Wales, the Green Party was elevated in the national consciousness from a fringe, amateur outfit to a more established fixture within the party system.

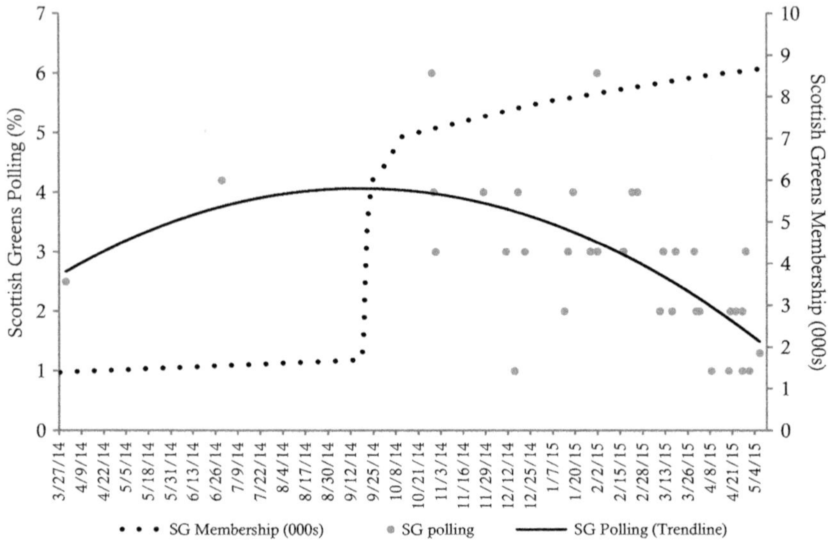

Fig. 1.3 The polling and membership of the Scottish Greens, 2014–2015 (Source: www.electoralcalculus.co.uk, British Election Study, www.scottishgreens.org.uk)

An Unlikely Rise

Until 2015, Britain's Green parties had consistently performed poorly in general elections. Neither the GPEW nor the Scottish Greens had ever won more than 1.1 per cent of the vote. Although the GPEW's vote share had risen from just 0.2 per cent in 1997 to just over 1 per cent in 2005, the 2010 election actually saw the Greens' vote share fall. In contrast, by the mid-2000s numerous other European Green parties had participated in government while Greens in other parts of the English-speaking world regularly achieved vote shares at national elections of double figures.

The Greens' rapid increase in membership–threefold in England and Wales and eightfold in Scotland–looks particularly puzzling when compared to recent trends in party membership in advanced democracies. Indeed, a secular decline in party membership across Europe was considered to be "unequivocal" just a few years earlier (Mair 2013: 40). In the UK, total party membership had fallen by 66 per cent between 1980 and 2009, leading the BBC to ask "Can UK political parties be saved from extinction?"[3] Contradicting these pessimistic predictions, in the nine months prior to the 2015 General Election nearly 60,000 citizens joined Britain's two Green parties.

Moreover, the experience of the Greens in 2014 and 2015 contradicts the prevalent idea that citizens are increasingly detached from politics. Typically, Mair (2013: 42–44) argued that "citizens are withdrawing and disengaging from the arena of conventional politics." Not only did the Greens' membership increase, but their growth was at least partially the result of efforts from highly engaged citizens. In autumn of 2014, nearly 300,000 Britons signed an online petition calling for the GPEW's inclusion in the pre-election televised leaders' debates, essentially forcing the broadcasters to reverse their previous decision to exclude the party.[4] The GPEW was able to raise nearly £300,000 from small-scale donations, via the website Crowdfunder. Arguably, the recent history of the Greens challenges the notion that "the age of party democracy has passed" (Mair 2013: 18).

Finally, the 2015 General Election had some of the qualities that we would normally associate with a particularly unfavourable political context for the Greens. In the approach to the election, it was unclear which of the two major parties would form the next government, which, coupled with Britain's majoritarian electoral system, should have acted as a strong incentive against voting for a small party. Furthermore, the Greens' left-wing voters should have been particularly mobilised to coalesce around the Labour Party after its move to the left on economic issues during the Parliament. Finally, the issue of the environment and climate change were overshadowed throughout the Parliament by topics such as austerity, immigration and health while the Greens were still perceived by the electorate in 2014 as a single-issue environmentalist organisation. No wonder one GPEW member reflected after the election, "what has happened in this last year or two is quite stunningly interesting, but I still can't quite figure it out."

Explaining the Rise of the Greens in Britain

To explain the rise of the Greens in Britain, I consider Britain's political context, the party's evolving political message, the reconfiguration of its internal organisation and personnel, the growth of its resources, the party's leadership and policy offer and, finally, its communications strategy and national and constituency campaigns. I also explore the motivations of the Greens' voters and the determinants of Green Party constituency-level success.

This study will draw on multiple data sources. The primary source is the 2014–2017 British Election Study (BES), which includes the responses of over 40,000 individuals–1,419 of whom voted Green–to extensive political surveys.[5] Of particular use to this study, most of the respondents were asked questions repeatedly over six waves between February 2014 and May 2015, allowing for the analysis of political dynamics as they were happening and perfectly encompassing the time period in which the Greens' growth took place. To understand the simultaneous events happening within the party, forty interviews were held between September 2015 and January 2016 with leading members and candidates of the GPEW, the Scottish Greens and the Green Party in Northern Ireland. These interviews were held face to face and over the phone, with some sections of the interviews done on a confidential basis at the request of the interviewee. Furthermore, fifty other Green Party parliamentary candidates were asked to evaluate their campaign and offer their opinions on changes in the party via e-mail surveys; around a quarter obliged. In addition, the profile of the Green Party's changing membership is analysed using data from the Party Members Project, which comprises both surveys and in-depth interviews to better understand the composition, motivations, opinions and activities of the six largest British parties, including the GPEW.[6] Data from an assortment of other surveys, such as those by YouGov, Survation and Lord Ashcroft polls, are also evaluated. Other sources are also employed, such as internal Green Party documents, news articles, the Chapel Hill Expert Survey (CHES) and the Qualitative Election Study of Britain (QESB).[7,8] Overall, these sources provide both a broad, quantitative view of the electorate, the Green Party's voters and its members and detailed qualitative insights into the experiences of the Green Party's leadership and candidates.

The book proceeds as follows. In Chapter 2, I show that between 2010 and 2015 the Greens had an increasingly distinct and resonant political message thanks to the entry of the Liberal Democrats into government, the leadership of Labour under Ed Miliband, the rise of UKIP and continuing changes in the Green Party's policies and ideology. In Chapter 3, I consider how the European and local election results of 2014 offered the Greens, the media and others an opportunity to cast the party as an increasingly relevant electoral force and a potential 'UKIP of the

Left'. I also investigate internal changes in the party's structure, staffing and operations, which I analyse and compare to other European Green parties. Finally, the effect of the Scottish Independence referendum on the Scottish Greens is assessed, including quantitative analyses to explain why the Greens underwent their membership boom following the referendum. Chapter 4 covers the Green Surge in England and Wales of late 2014 and early 2015. I explain why the GPEW underwent a dramatic uptick in members and poll ratings and consider the effect that this period had on the party's ideological positioning and finances. Chapter 5 documents the subsequent decline in the Greens' poll ratings. Particular attention is paid to the party's leadership, its policy offer and its national and constituency election campaigns. Chapters 6 and 7 look back on the election and offer analytical models that explain variance in individual party choice–why some voters chose the Greens and some did not–and variance in constituency results–why the Greens did well in some areas and less well in others.

Notes

1. Most polling companies treat the entirely independent GPEW and the Scottish Greens as one party for the purposes of national polls.
2. Ofcom (2015), 'Review of Ofcom list of major political parties for elections taking place on 7 May 2015', accessed at http://stakeholders.ofcom.org.uk/binaries/consultations/major-parties-15/statement/Major_Parties_Statement.pdf on 21/06/2016.
3. Wheeler, B. (2011), 'Can UK political parties be saved from extinction?', accessed at http://www.bbc.co.uk/news/uk-politics-12934148 on 24/01/2016.
4. Standard Reporter (2015), 'Green Party invited to join election TV debates under new plans', accessed at http://www.standard.co.uk/news/politics/broadcasters-revise-debates-plans-to-include-the-green-party-9996798.html on 24/01/2016.
5. Fieldhouse, E., J. Green., G. Evans., H. Schmitt, C. van der Eijk, J. Mellon & C. Prosser (2015) British Election Study Internet Panel Waves 1-6. DOI: 10.15127/1.293723.
6. T. Bale, P. Webb & M. Poletti (2015), ESRC Party Members Project (PMP), UK Party Membership Survey 2015, Round 1.
7. Ryan Bakker, Erica Edwards, Liesbet Hooghe, Seth Jolly, Gary Marks, Jonathan Polk, Jan Rovny, Marco Steenbergen, and Milada Vachudova. 2015. "2014 Chapel Hill Expert Survey." Version 2015.1. Available on chesdata.eu. Chapel Hill, NC: University of North Carolina, Chapel Hill.

8. Carvalho, E. and K. Winters. 2015. 'The Qualitative Election Study of Britain 2015 Dataset', version 1.0. Funded by British Academy and Leverhulme Small Grant SG142740 and supported by GESIS, Carnegie Corporation, and University of Dundee. Available at: http://wintersresearch.wordpress.com

Bibliography

Mair, P. (2013), *Ruling The Void: The Hollowing of Western Democracy*, London: Verso

CHAPTER 2

Usual Low in an Increasingly Favourable Context

Abstract Despite flatlining in terms of poll ratings, membership and exposure between the 2010 General Election and the 2014 European Election, the major political events of this period offered the Greens an unprecedented opportunity to appeal to voters. Of particular importance was the entry of the Liberal Democrats into government, which robbed that party of its protest image and exposed an ideological divide between its leadership and supporters. Ed Miliband's leadership of the Labour Party, which I argue sent an ambiguous message on the two issues of austerity and immigration, and the increasing anti-immigration sentiment in the wider public–culminating in the rise of the populist right party, UKIP–also gave the Greens' message particular relevance. By 2010 the historically under-performing Greens had already coalesced around a left-wing and more socio-economic, rather than environmental, message. However, the austerity programme of the coalition government gave this message a focal point and accorded the Greens' protesting image mainstream relevance as it emerged as the best placed party to attract anti-establishment left-wing voters.

Keywords Green Party • Liberal Democrats • Labour • UKIP • Economy • Austerity • Immigration • Populism

Despite laying claim to being the oldest environmentalist party in Europe, the Greens in Britain have been consistently outperformed in national

J. Dennison, *The Greens in British Politics*,
DOI 10.1007/978-3-319-42673-0_2

elections by their sister parties in other advanced democracies. Whereas no British Green party had ever secured more than 1.1 per cent of the general election vote before 2015, a combination of more favourable electoral systems, state funding and, often, stronger domestic anti-nuclear and '1968' movements had, by the late 1980s, given the German, Belgian, Swedish, Finnish and Austrian Green parties relative successes in national elections of, generally, between four and nine per cent of the national vote. Furthermore, by the end of the 1990s, the five European Green parties had participated in national government and, in 2004, the first European Green Prime Minister was elected in Latvia.

Whereas the national electoral performances of the GPEW and Scottish Greens had been, until 2015, relatively poor, from 1999 onwards they had both experienced greater success in the more proportional elections to the European Parliament and the newly formed Scottish Parliament and Welsh Assembly, as well as the London Assembly since its creation in 2000. In particular, the Greens had done well in European elections, which arguably suit the Greens' environmentalist and post-national narrative, and London Assembly elections, partially because of London's Green-friendly demographics (see Fig. 2.1). In the Scottish and Welsh elections, Greens have faced obvious competition from similarly left-libertarian nationalist parties.

The stark difference between the Greens' general election performances and results in more proportional elections strongly suggests that the electoral system singularly explains the GPEW and Scottish Greens' historic inability to make a convincing breakthrough at Westminster. However, the cross-country evidence weakens this argument. First, the Canadian Greens, the only Green party competing in an identical first-past-the-post Westminster system, have, in each of the last five elections, received between four and seven per cent of the vote. Similarly, prior to New Zealand's 1993 electoral reform, the Green Party of New Zealand had managed to secure seven per cent of the vote. In the USA, nearly three per cent of the electorate voted Green in the 2000 Presidential Election. Even in Britain, the, still unified, Green Party won 15 per cent of the vote and came in third place in the, still first-past-the-post, 1989 European Parliament election. More recently, the GPEW have gradually increased their vote share and seats in local elections, which use first-past-the-post, since the late 1990s (see Fig. 2.1).

Why, then, did the Greens in Britain do relatively poorly at general elections prior to 2015? Part of the answer lies in the party's extraordinary

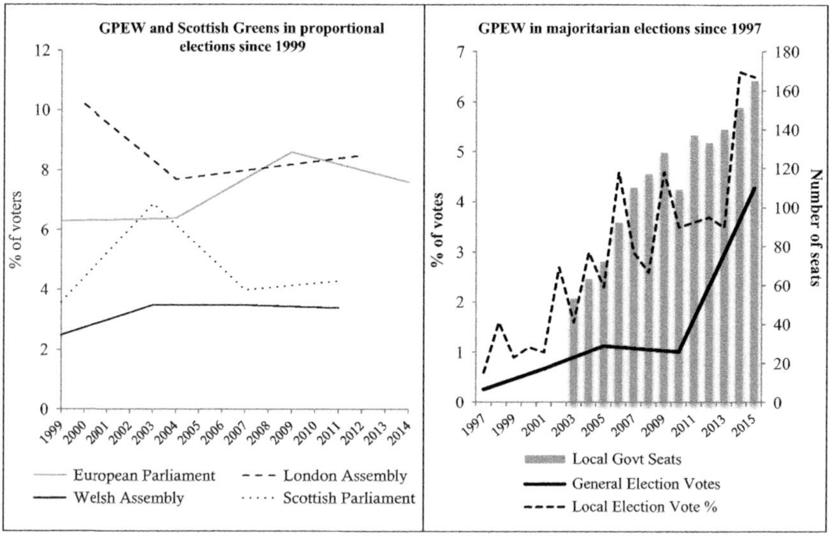

Fig. 2.1 GPEW and Scottish Green recent electoral history in proportional elections (*left*) and majoritarian elections (*right*) (Note: European Parliament vote share combines votes for the GPEW and the Scottish Greens; Welsh Assembly and Scottish Parliament vote share considers only the Regional and not Constituency vote share)

European election result of 1989. In that year, the Greens had a monopoly over their environmentalist message, which focussed on pollutants in the water and food supply, conservation, nuclear waste and the greenhouse effect, as well as criticism of the European Community's democratic deficit in anticipation of the much-heralded creation of the single market in 1992, as evidenced by their widely acclaimed 1989 party political broadcasts.[1] The party's approach could be summarised by the German Greens' slogan of 'neither left nor right but ahead' (Capra and Spretnak 1984). Peter Barnett, a three-time member of the Green Party National Executive (GPEx)–the annually elected committee responsible for day-to-day running of the party–remembers, "When I joined the party in '88, I was quite right-wing ... all the party's ecological and environmental politics was very, very neutral at that time, you could knock on anybody's door and you'd always get very welcomed." This environmentalist message was particularly relevant in the late 1980s, as a post-Chernobyl 'Green Tide' swept over Europe, perhaps best evidenced by Margaret Thatcher in 1989 addressing the United Nations General Assembly to express her view that "of all the challenges faced by the world community [...] one has grown clearer than any other in both urgency and importance – I refer to the threat to our global environment."[2]

The resonance of the Greens' message in 1989 meant that they were the natural choice for voters unconvinced by either the Conservatives or Labour after the SDP-Liberal Alliance broke down. This centrist alliance, which had won nearly 20 per cent of the vote in the previous European election, collapsed in 1988 amidst acrimonious, though eventually successful, attempts to fully merge its two constituent parties. The newly formed party, still recovering from in-fighting, was unable to run a fully-fledged campaign and saw its vote share reduced to just six per cent. The Greens were thus an attractive proposition due to their inclusive message and lack of competition from what would become the Liberal Democrats. Twenty-five years later, even Nigel Farage, leader of UKIP, would admit that he voted Green in 1989.[3]

It was this success that ironically robbed the Greens of their distinctive message and led to bitter in-fighting. The 1989 result encouraged both the Conservatives and Labour to incorporate environmentalism into their policies and rhetoric, creating hitherto non-existent 'green' competition for the Green Party. Increasing air and water quality became part of government policy, both at the national and European level, with impressive success.[4] Furthermore, the resurrected Liberal Democrats rapidly rose to become the protest vote of choice for voters on both left and right, as well as securing their own heartlands in the West Country, Scotland and Wales.

The UK Green Party, which lacked the infrastructure to capture potential members in the wake of its 1989 success, quickly returned to its tiny polling figures after dividing, on friendly terms, into three parties–for England and Wales, Scotland and Northern Ireland, respectively–and spending the following years mired by ideological in-fighting between 'realists and fundamentalists' (Burchell 2002). Almost the entire party leadership resigned in the early 1990s after grass roots members rallied against their attempts to turn the party into a more election-focussed organisation. Eventually, these developments forced the Greens–which began to resemble an NGO more than an orthodox party–to find a political home to the left of the major parties, depriving them of the opportunity to again be the catch-all party they were in 1989 (Dennison 2015: 190). At the 1997 General

Election the GPEW gained its lowest vote share since 1983, while less than 2,000 people voted for the Scottish Greens north of the border.

At the turn of the millennium, the Greens were, in economic terms, a clearly left-wing political party. The 1999 CHES (Chapel Hill Expert Survey) placed the GPEW at 1.9 on their 0–10 left-right economic axis and 1.8 on their libertarian-authoritarian axis. In 2001 the party's manifesto called for a Citizen's Income and higher taxes and spending. However, at this point, the party's economic policies were given far less prominence than its environmental and quality of life policies. The party's 2001 manifesto only mentioned economics after deploring the rise in car traffic and the UK's disappointing recycling figures. Furthermore, the party's economic stance was highly 'post-material' (Inglehart 1971), expressing their scepticism towards economic growth with the passage "the costs of our increasingly stressful and over-industrialised way of life outweigh the material advances of the last thirty years."[5] Such post-material arguments tended to fall on deaf ears in the UK, which lacked the strong 1968 movements of continental Europe (Nehring 2008: 130) and continued to vote more according to economic issues– as opposed to identity issues–than other western European countries (Kriesi et al. 2008).

Throughout the 2000s, the GPEW gradually gave economic issues greater prominence and expressed their views in more classically left-wing, 'materialist' terms. Following the party's 2007 decision to have a single party leader, rather than one male and one female 'Principal Speaker', both of its elected leaders–Caroline Lucas and Natalie Bennett–have described themselves as socialists.[6] Darren Hall, 2015 Green parliamentary candidate for Bristol West, argues that "the internal change in terms of policy was really driven by Caroline Lucas [...] and then handing over the Natalie who continued that process of social *and* environmental justice." *Green Left*, an internal 'anti-capitalist and eco-socialist' party group, was founded in 2006 and quickly became one of the more powerful groups within the GPEW. Furthermore, the GPEW's increased involvement in electoral competition forced it to give economic issues more prevalence. Caroline Lucas, the Greens' first MP, says that in Brighton "we worked a lot on that before 2010, because the few places where we'd been able to afford to do focus groups told us very clearly that they really liked what we were saying about the environment, but they wanted to know where we stood on the economy so we made much more of an effort to talk about those issues."

The GPEW's success in winning seats in the European Parliament and devolved assemblies, from 1999 onwards, gave the party its first public exposure since the 1980s. Darren Johnson, Green Member of the London Assembly (MLA), states that "from day one there's been a Green presence in City Hall. We've been really quite focused in how we can use that as a platform to promote the issues we care about and promote the party." Caroline Lucas' 2010 victory in Brighton offered the party far greater exposure still. Lucas took part in numerous demonstrations against the government's austerity programme, most notably as part of the People's Assembly Against Austerity, and, quite incredibly, against the Brighton & Hove City Council, which had in 2011 become the UK's first Green Party–run council and was required to impose public spending cuts of £26 million. In 2013, Lucas was reprimanded for wearing a 'No More Page Three' t-shirt in the chamber of the House of Commons as part of a campaign against photos of bare-breasted women in tabloid newspapers. In the same year, Lucas was arrested at a protest against fracking of shale gas in Sussex. Rupert Read, long-time Green campaigner and 2015 GPEW candidate for Cambridge, reflects that Lucas's "increased profile as an MP, and perhaps the best known Green Party representative, really showcased our value set and demonstrated that we have the competence to implement it." Lucas's actions as a parliamentarian underlined the Greens' identity as highly anti-establishment, anti-austerity and anti-capitalist, in contrast to the centrism of the party in 1989, when a plurality of its voters were ex-Conservatives (Richardson and Rootes 1995: 73).

The internal 'anti-capitalist' march of the party accelerated after 2010 as a younger generation of members joined, many of whom had been involved in student and anti-austerity protests after the coalition government took power. As shown in Chapter 4, the members that joined between 2010 and 2013 were more radical than those that joined either before or afterwards. The party's transformation was completed at its 2013 Spring Conference. There, 71 per cent of delegates voted to replace the preamble to the party's constitution with a version, penned by university students, that committed the GPEW to the "transformation of society for the benefit of the many not the few."[7] Left-wing blog Left Foot Forward predicted the "constitutional amendment should help strengthen their position as the only significant party to the left of Labour." One older GPEW member expressed his frustration at this change with a message on the party's message board that read "Environmental issues side-lined. Overdevelopment on green field land ignored by national spokespeople.

All public pronouncements on socio-economic policies to the left of the Labour Party. Population growth ignored as an issue. Anti-roads campaigning not a priority. Left-wing spending pledges that haven't been fully costed. Has the party that was once 'The Ecology Party' been hijacked by people who wish to turn it into the Michael Foot era Labour Party circa 1982?"[8] Such members were now heavily outnumbered in the party.

Following this constitutional amendment, during the 2013 local elections GPEW leader Natalie Bennett focussed largely on opposition to public spending cuts. When Bennett was asked in a BBC interview why people should care about environmental issues at a time of economic crisis, she replied, "we are speaking up for a different kind of economy [...] we are saying globalisation and neo-liberalism has hit its limits. We are saying we need strong local economies built around small businesses and shops. We are speaking up for a whole range of things and speaking against the government's cuts and speaking up for proper services."[9] Though traces of post-materialist language remained, the GPEW's focus was clearly on opposition to spending cuts. "We as a party made a conscious decision", says Keith Taylor MEP, "we decided that the threats from austerity and the conditions affecting the most vulnerable society actually warranted action."

Despite such pronouncements, the electorate remained ignorant of the GPEW's non-environmental positions. When asked where the Greens stood on government redistribution of incomes, with zero being most in favour and ten being most against, in May 2014 the public answered on average that the Greens were around 3.8, further to the right than Labour (British Election Study 2014–2017). The most common perception of the Greens' economic stance was that they were squarely centrist–five on the scale. By contrast, one year later, the most common response would be zero and the average response, 2.8, putting the GPEW well to the left of Labour. Party insiders were aware of the lack of public knowledge on the Greens' economic policies. "The two stereotypes that held the Green Party back for so long were that, one, we were a single issue party that was only about the environment and, two, we could never win election", argues Darren Johnson, Green MLA. Natalie Bennett explains that "we'd always struggled to get those messages out, and indeed, in the first year or so of my leadership, when I went on the BBC, there was usually a picture of a polar bear, a wind turbine, or on really good days, a waste tube behind me. It was very, very hard." Darren Hall, Green candidate for Bristol West, argues that clarifying their economic stances was the GPEW's biggest job after 2010: "the last five years in the Green Party was all about trying to make people aware that we weren't a single issue party and in particular that meant taking on a much more obvious stance on things like low wages, nationalisation of the rail system, the NHS, equality issues, foreign crises overseas, those kinds of things."

Although the Green Party had expressed strong concerns about social justice and inequality since at least the 1990s, it was only after 2000 that economic issues began to become the primary concern of the party. This transformation was completed after the beginning of the coalition government's austerity programme in 2010, which gave the party an unprecedented opportunity for political relevance and drew a new, young generation of radical, anti-capitalists members towards the Greens who, with a single MP and a presence in devolved assemblies and the European Parliament, were best placed to take on the mantle of the UK's primary anti-austerity party.

Coalition, Cuts and Compliance

The 2010 General Election resulted in no party having an overall majority. In the hope that his party would benefit from a bidding war over the terms of a coalition agreement, Nick Clegg, leader of the Liberal Democrats, entered into negotiations with both Labour and the Conservatives. This strategy reaped some rewards; the Liberal Democrats won 22 per cent of cabinet seats despite only having 16 per cent of the new government's MPs. However, the high-profile negotiations portrayed the decision to enter into coalition with the Conservatives, rather than Labour, as an ideological choice instead of a political necessity, which the arithmetic of the House of Commons suggested it actually was. The Coalition Agreement, which outlined the new government's programme, stated that both parties held the "conviction that the days of big government are over; that centralisation and top-down control have proved a failure."[10] Moreover, Liberal Democrats in government blamed Britain's economic woes primarily on high public spending, rather than under-regulation of the banking sector or exogenous economic events. As a result, the new government committed itself to reducing 80 per cent of the fiscal deficit via public spending cuts, with just 20 per cent being eliminated via tax increases.

The Lib Dems' early actions in government were in clear contrast to the beliefs of their 2010 voters who described themselves as left wing rather than right wing at a rate of four to one (British Election Study 2010).

Indeed, many voters had historically opted for the Liberal Democrats precisely to keep the Conservatives out of power in constituencies with little Labour presence (Cutts and Russell 2015: 80). The Coalition Agreement inadvertently exposed the ideological distance between the party's classically liberal, pro-market leadership, known as the Orange Bookers, and its social democrat grass roots membership and voters.

The framing of the coalition by both parties–a government in the 'national interest' at a time of 'economic emergency'–precluded any opportunity for the Liberal Democrats to distinguish themselves from the Conservatives on the key issue of deficit reduction via austerity. The Liberal Democrats failed to find a way to overcome the 'unity-distinctiveness dilemma' that faces all junior coalition partners, who must "maximise governmental effectiveness while at the same time protecting the identity and distinctiveness" and, thus, their electoral relevance (Hazell and Yong 2012: 7). By reducing the government's mission to the singular statistic of Britain's fiscal deficit, the Liberal Democrats' individual achievements became indiscernible to the electorate from those of the Conservatives. In government, Clegg did little to break with the adversarialist traditions of British politics, consistently focussing early attacks on Labour rather than the Conservatives with repeated allusions to cleaning up 'Labour's economic mess'.[11] The nature of the coalition and its aims quickly made it difficult for the Liberal Democrats to distinguish themselves from their coalition partners.

The Liberal Democrats also lost public trust because of their agreement to increase university tuition fees despite having campaigned heavily to remove them altogether prior to the 2010 General Election. This volte-face was probably not the cause of the Liberal Democrat polling collapse; the party was already languishing at eight per cent in the polls prior to the tuition fees announcement. The importance of the tuition fees decision was that it offered detractors of the party a point of attack and meant that no major party would be offering the policy of no university tuition fees in 2015, a proposal seen as key to winning the votes of students. "I voted Lib Dem at the last election and of course then I was completely let down and I thought 'I'm never going to vote tactically again, it's values all the way'", said a young newcomer to the Bristol Green Party in 2015, while another remembered "the fact that the Lib Dems broke their promise really made me angry. It made me want to do something about it."[12]

By February 2014, only 25 per cent of Britons who had voted for the Liberal Democrats in 2010 were planning to stay loyal to Clegg's party in 2015 (British Election Study 2014–2017). Those ex-Lib Dems seeking a centre-left party with a realistic chance of defeating the Conservatives turned towards Labour. On the other hand, those seeking a "radical, progressive party" instead of a "split the difference centre party" would turn elsewhere.[13] The division of ex-Liberal Democrats between radicals and centrists had a profound effect on the Green Party's final vote share. Half of 2015 Green voters had voted for the Liberal Democrats in 2010 and the figure is even higher when 2015 first-time voters are discounted (British Election Study 2014–2017). Similarly, 29 per cent of 2015 Green voters opted for the Liberal Democrats in 2005, a figure that rises to 44 per cent when those ineligible to vote at the time are excluded. In terms of past party choice, disgruntled Lib Dems were the primary source for Green Party voters in 2015.

In response to their polling collapse, the Liberal Democrats adopted two key strategies, both of which are likely to have ultimately aided the Green Party. First, without a clear socio-demographic base and robbed of their historic campaigning reliance on protest votes and popular leadership, the party turned to local issues as the way to save their still numerous MPs (Cutts and Russell 2015: 73). Indeed, 2015 Liberal Democrat voters were more likely than the average voter to prefer their MP to focus on constituency issues rather than national issues, whereas the opposite was the case for ex-Liberal Democrat Green voters (British Election Study 2014–2017). Greens are "interested in big picture, broad, international-type policy issues", reflects one Green Party councillor. The Liberal Democrats' strategy of focusing on local matters, though possibly effective for their overall vote share, probably harmed them disproportionately with voters sympathetic to the Green Party's globalist message.

Second, the Liberal Democrats' collapsed poll ratings forced them to campaign according to a "strongly defensive targeting strategy with resources concentrated in incumbent seats, primarily those that had sitting MPs and where the local party had remained active for a sustained period during the electoral cycle" (Cutts and Russell 2015: 76). The retreat of Nick Clegg's party meant that vast tracts of the country opened up for a left-libertarian party. One of these seats–Norwich South–had been a key Green target constituency since at least 2005. In another, Totnes, where the Liberal Democrat vote fell from 36 per cent in 2010 to 10 per cent in 2015, "the Lib Dem knew that he wasn't going to get in because of what happened to the national vote", remembers Gill Coombs, the Green Party parliamentary candidate for Totnes

The signing of the Coalition Agreement by the Conservative and Liberal Democrat parties in May 2010, the first of its kind in Britain since the 1930s, was perhaps the single most important event in explaining the rise of the Greens in Britain. Nick Clegg, leader of the Liberal Democrats, justified his party's entry into the Coalition as a response to a national economic emergency in which the fiscal deficit had to be reduced. In doing so, he fused the aims, agency and accomplishments of his party in government with those of the Conservatives, robbing his party of the distinctiveness necessary to retain a viable electoral appeal. Fiscal conservatism alienated left-wing Liberal Democrat voters and austerity became the natural focus for anti-government campaigns. The Liberal Democrat strategy of targeting all of its resources towards defending its strongest incumbent MPs and campaigning on local issues would both turn off potential Green voters and leave many parts of the country without a left-libertarian party campaigning on the ground. Ultimately, those former Liberal Democrats who were most concerned with ousting the Conservatives from government could turn towards the competitive, if unspectacular, Labour Party while more radically minded voters would be forced to look elsewhere.

The Labour Party and Mr Milibiguous

By 2014, the Green Party's major competitor for votes was no longer the Liberal Democrats but was instead the Labour Party. Of those who eventually voted Green in the 2015 General Election, 25 per cent had intended to vote Labour when asked in February 2014, only slightly fewer than the 28 per cent who had already decided to vote Green (British Election Study 2014–2017).[14] Furthermore, of those who said that they intended to vote Green *at any* point between February 2014 and May 2015, Labour was the second most likely *actual* vote choice at 24 per cent, after the 55 per cent who ultimately did vote Green but far ahead of the eight per cent who opted for the Liberal Democrats.[15] In the year and a half prior to the General Election, Labour was the party from whom the Greens took the most voters and to whom they lost the most voters, with the former outnumbering the latter at a rate of two to one.

In some ways Labour in 2015 should have been very well placed to take Green voters. Not only was its leader, 'Red' Ed Miliband, seen as a move to the left for the party but he was also the former Secretary of State for Energy and Climate Change, during which time he legislated to cut greenhouse gases by 80 per cent and was seen as a determined environmentalist.[16] One environmental website speculated that Miliband would use green topics to "put much clear water" between himself and the Coalition and that already he had "won a lot of friends in the environmental movement."[17] Moreover, the polling collapse of the centre-left Liberal Democrats upon their entry to government offered Labour the chance to unite left-wing voters in the face of an austerity-driven government and the majoritarian Westminster electoral system. In 2011, Miliband issued a "rallying call" to former Liberal Democrat voters who, like him, saw the coalition as a "tragic choice" and he explicitly aimed to unite Britain's "progressive majority."[18]

However, after thirteen years in power and three consecutive outright election victories, returning to opposition had not been straightforward for either Labour or its new leader. The party failed to find a convincing narrative after the highly centrist and pro-business New Labour period, which Miliband declared to be "over".[19] Simultaneously, the Labour Party was unable to acquit itself of accusations of guilt for Britain's high fiscal deficit and the financial crisis moreover. The Conservatives repeatedly claimed that Labour had "maxed out the nation's credit card" and that any proposed alternatives to austerity were proof that Miliband and his team were "deficit deniers" (Gamble 2015: 158).[20] Essentially, the party found itself in a rhetorical Catch-22 whereby moves away from the New Labour period, which almost by default were leftward on economic matters, reinforced an image of fiscal irresponsibility, whereas accepting the coalition's austerity narrative would entail admitting blame for the economic crisis.

Labour's response to this conundrum was essentially a move leftwards on all economic policy *except* the key issue of the day–how to reduce Britain's fiscal deficit–resulting in a muddled, ambiguous message. Labour produced a long list of left-wing and generally popular new policies such as cutting tuition fees, reintroduction of the 50 per cent tax rate, an energy price freeze, challenging tax avoiders, an increase in the minimum wage, rent capping and breaking up the big banks (Cowley and Kavanagh 2015: 79, 81). However, on the issue of the fiscal deficit, Miliband and his Shadow Chancellor, Ed Balls, felt compelled to follow the coalition's course of austerity. In January 2013, Balls announced that a Labour government would not reverse most of the government's cuts. In June, he promised to follow the Coalition's spending plans for 2015–2016 and at the end of that year he imposed a zero-based spending review whereby Labour ministers would not be able to promise new spending without offering equivalent savings elsewhere.[21] Labour's proposed £2.5 billion spending increase on the NHS was dwarfed by that of the Conservatives who promised to increase NHS funding by £8 billion (Fielding 2015: 66). Attempts at appearing fiscally responsible were simultaneously confused by Miliband addressing the People's Assembly Against Austerity and marching with the Trade Union Congress against cuts in public spending (Cowley and Kavanagh 2015: 92). This ambiguity is displayed in Fig. 2.2, in which we can see a slight leftward move on overall economic matters by Labour between 2010 and 2014, yet on the specific issue of higher taxes versus lower spending, a sharp move to the right.

Beyond economics, the intellectual underpinnings of Miliband's rhetoric tended to come from the 'Blue Labour' approach of Maurice Glasman. Whereas New Labour balanced its pro-market approach with progressive policies on issues such as constitutional reform, multiculturalism, immigration and, by British standards, European integration, 'Blue Labour' was more suspicious of the market and called for a renewed appeal to the identity, localist, patriotic and anti-immigration sentiments that it believed were core to blue-collar attitudes. In mid-2012, as Labour became increasingly concerned by the rise of UKIP,

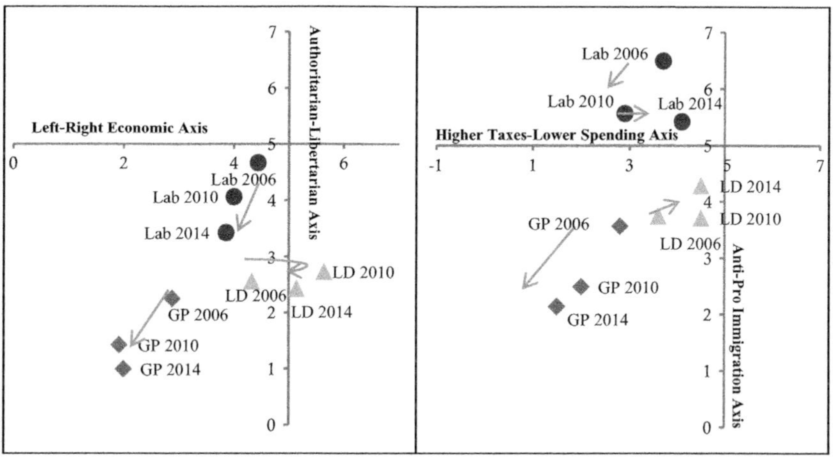

Fig. 2.2 Party positions on overall economic and social matters (*left*) and on the specific issues of tax and spending and immigration (*right*) (Source: Chapel Hill Experts Survey 1999–2014 Trend File)

Miliband said that New Labour had "got it wrong" on immigration.[22] Moreover, the party attempted to rebrand itself with overarching slogans of 'One Nation Labour' and a commitment to the 'British Promise', both of which attempted to put a soft nationalism at the centre of Labour's messaging.

To some of those on the left, greater use of nationalistic rhetoric represented a clear regressive step. "Labour was so compromised in terms of the message it was getting out", Caroline Lucas argues, "it wasn't clearly anti-austerity. It wasn't clearly standing up for migrants [...] They never properly challenged the Conservative lie that the financial crisis was caused by their record rather than by an international banking crisis. So our message was very resonant [...] here was a party that wasn't ducking and weaving depending on what we thought public opinion was. We were standing up for migrants." Although its anti-immigration policy manoeuvres were minor, Labour ultimately headlined its immigration strategy simply, if vacuously, as 'controls on immigration'. "When I left the Labour Party, they hadn't got a clear policy platform at all, so there wasn't very much for me to go on. What I could go on was the language that they were using: Growth-driven, the focus on work, on strivers, on cutting the deficit", remembers ex-Labour Party member Matt Hawkins, now Media Officer for the London Green Party, "there seemed to be no alternative or grand vision that they were offering."

By 2014, Miliband's early preoccupation with moving his party beyond New Labour, typically to the left on economic issues, had given way to awkward attempts to portray his party as fiscally responsible and, increasingly, receptive to concerns over immigration. The result was that Labour under Ed Miliband moved to the left on all economic issues *except* austerity, over which it jolted to the right. As occurred in other European countries with austerity programmes, such as Spain, Portugal and Greece, the major centre-left party lost support in the latter half of the Parliament as centrists perceived them to be an economic risk while leftists were contemptuous of their meek challenge to the austerity narrative. There was now a broad and otherwise unoccupied space on the political spectrum for an anti-austerity, pro-immigration party to exploit. Ultimately, Labour's diffidence on these two key matters would only highlight the Green Party's explicit and sweeping anti-austerity, globalist and left-wing rhetoric.

The UKIPisation of British Politics

Between 2005 and 2015, the rise in public disquiet about immigration, extremism and segregated communities, as well as the resulting growth of the British National Party and, later, the more pronounced growth of the UK Independence Party, led all three of Britain's mainstream political parties to move away from their earlier commitments to multiculturalism and immigration. In 2005, Britain's political consensus was a diluted version of much of what Green Party voters wanted. Throughout the preceding seven years, Labour, still under Tony Blair, had raised taxes and public spending, relaxed immigration law, established proportionally elected devolved assemblies, introduced rights for homosexuals, banned fox hunting and pursued closer European integration. In 2004, Blair gave a keynote speech on the need for the UK government to tackle climate change, underlining Britain's leadership on tackling climate change.[23]

If left-wing voters had misgivings about Labour, they could vote for the high-flying Liberal Democrats who, under the leadership of social democrat Charles Kennedy, initially opposed the Iraq War, supported greater civil liberties, backed the UK joining the euro, and campaigned for electoral reform and open government.[24] On top of this, three consecutive electoral losses were enough to convince the Conservatives that they too should follow the Blairite consensus and so elected David Cameron, the self-described 'Heir to Blair', as Conservative leader.[25] For Cameron, "rather than focus on traditional right-wing themes such as immigration and Europe, which had failed his predecessors and damaged his party, he talked instead about tackling climate change, alleviating poverty, delivering overseas aid, legalizing same-sex marriage, celebrating Britain's ethnic diversity, and bringing more women and ethnic minorities into politics" (Goodwin and Milazzo 2015: 22).

By 2015, the tone of British politics was more similar to a soft version of what UKIP voters would want. Having witnessed the rise of UKIP, as well as increasing public anger over immigration, the three major British parties recalibrated their messaging on immigration, the EU and multiculturalism (Dennison and Goodwin 2015). Following the 7/7 terrorist attacks, Tony Blair increasingly disclaimed multiculturalism and his successor, Gordon Brown, sought to strengthen 'Britishness'. Whereas 1998 saw three British Prime Ministers, the Queen and Prince Charles describe the UK as a "proud multicultural nation", in late 2010 and early 2011, David Cameron, Angela Merkel, Nicolas Sarkozy, John Howard and Jose Maria Aznar all declared that multiculturalism had failed.[26, 27]

The about-turn in policy terms was reflected in the tone that mainstream parties took towards UKIP–in 2006 David Cameron had dismissed UKIP as "closet racists" yet by 2014 Ed Miliband had to explicitly deny that he thought Farage was a racist. "After working hard to dispel the perception that Labour regards anyone concerned about immigration as a bigot", commented the *New Statesman*, "it is not hard to see why Miliband is reluctant to attack the UKIP leader in such terms."[28] The hardened stance on immigration would be reflected in all three parties' 2015 election manifestos, which included lists of policies designed to reduce net migration levels. As Jean Lambert, Green MEP for London, summarises, "there was a competition about who could be the most restrictive."

Academics such as Bornschier and Kriesi (2012) argue that the debate over immigration forms part of an emerging cultural divide in advanced democracies over the nature of individuals and communities. Those inspired by 'New Left' thinkers of the 1970s seek to liberate the individual from oppression, not only in terms of class conflict but also from other unequal power relations, be they based on gender, sexuality, nationality or race. As such, traditional institutions, which were formed by and thus maintain those power structures, should be dismantled. To these thinkers, the pinnacle of such institutions is the nation state, which not only restricts individual liberty but also reinforces the notion of national difference, an affront to the universal nature of the individual. As this 'libertarian-universalist' view became more predominant throughout the late 20th century, opponents coalesced around a 'traditionalist-communitarian' standpoint (Bornschier 2010). To 'traditionalist-communitarians', individual identities are rooted in community traditions, which are inevitably particular and, thus, not universal. Efforts to remove traditions, overrule them via universalist initiatives or weaken the cultural homogeneity from which they arise are therefore an affront to the social nature of the individual. In policy terms, this dichotomy sees a preference for free movement of people and supranational government, on the one hand, and national sovereignty, homogeneity and closed borders on the other (Dennison and Goodwin 2015). Across much of Europe, the early 21st century sees this cultural divide–or 'integration-demarcation' axis– as almost as salient as the classic left-right divide over the distribution of material resources.

By 2015, the Conservatives, Labour and the Liberal Democrats had come to the view, to varying extents, that some 'traditionalist-communitarian' corrective was needed. However, 'libertarian-universalists' in the electorate remained, united by their pro-immigration, pro-multicultural and pro-internationalist beliefs. In 2014, though only six per cent of Britons believed that immigration should be increased, 32 per cent saw it as enriching British cultural life, 18 per cent believed that equal opportunities for ethnic minorities had not gone far enough and another 18 per cent believed that European unification should be pushed further.[29] These relatively small numbers explain why, to varying degrees, the major parties moved away from these positions. However, for the minority of Britons who remained 'libertarian-universalists', the rise of UKIP and the gravitational pull it exerted on the mainstream parties created the need for a left-wing counterweight.

UKIP's success was not only in the polls but also in terms of public interest. In the month of the 2013 local elections, there were more Google searches for UKIP than for the three mainstream parties combined.[30] At the time of the 2014 European Parliament elections, there were three times as many searches for UKIP as there were for the other parties. "In the run-up to the European election, Nigel Farage use to have to cough and he would make the six o'clock news", Keith Taylor, GPEW MEP, laments, concluding that "the increase in popularity for UKIP was media-constructed." Taylor's view is consistent with the timing of media supply and demand on UKIP–the proportion of online news articles mentioning UKIP to those mentioning any of the five parties in England and Wales was steady at 40 per cent from 2012 right up to the General Election, whereas public interest only really took off during the 2013 local elections and after the 2014 European election (source: LexisNexis, Google Trends). "Just how much media coverage does UKIP get?", asked two academics in the *New Statesman* in 2013, noting that "with 25 appearances by Nigel Farage on Question Time [the BBC's town hall-style political debate] and more than 23,000 press mentions, UKIP is attracting historically unprecedented levels of coverage for a minor party."[31] Even Farage triumphantly stated, "all they talk about is me."[32] The media had found a political subject that, eventually, drew in more of the public than the classic two-party horse race for No. 10. Moreover, that subject was less often UKIP's policy programme but was far more focused on their leader and their potential to undermine the pre-existing party system.

Psychologically, the rise of UKIP signalled the end of the previous two-and-a-half party system, in place for nearly 40 years. "I definitely think the rise of UKIP helped the Greens because it said that we weren't in three-party politics", says Darren Hall, Green candidate for Bristol West, "it demonstrated the fact that we can have more parties in national politics."

Pippa Bartolotti, leader of the Greens in Wales, agreed, noting, "by the time we got to the general election it was becoming accepted that politics was going to be messy, you weren't going to have a tidy panel of three people speaking, and that meant inclusiveness of UKIP." As would be best exemplified by the dispute over the televised leaders' debates, the rise of UKIP forced a re-examination of political institutions and opened the possibility for other parties to gain entry into the party system.

Moreover, UKIP benefited from an anti-establishment sentiment that existed in the public on both sides of the left-right spectrum, which could equally be exploited by other minor parties. "Certainly Nigel Farage is vigorous", admits Caroline Lucas MP, "whatever one thinks of his policies, and personally I absolutely hate them, he does a very good job of energetically challenging the other parties, and being that insurgent figure. Energetic in a way that to be honest Ed Miliband just wasn't – he just seemed to be incredibly uncomfortable with whatever compromise he was trying to bind together at any given point. And just like UKIP is uncompromising, I think the Greens were uncompromising in that sense." UKIP offered a prototype to other parties of how anti-establishment sentiment in the electorate could be harnessed through energetic and 'authentic' imagery and messages.

Chief among UKIP's messages was that a corrupt elite had betrayed the electorate. Farage dismissed domestic politicians, exclaiming, "we are run by a bunch of college kids who are completely untouched by the real people of this world."[33] UKIP's message was classically populist, arguing "society to be ultimately separated into two homogeneous and antagonistic groups, 'the pure people' versus 'the corrupt elite'" (Mudde 2004: 543). Though the historic link between populism and the right has often led to a conflation between populism and xenophobia, the rise of left-wing populists after 2010, such as Syriza in Greece and Podemos in Spain, who also used the pure people/corrupt elite dichotomy showed that populism could be fused with ideologies from both left and right.[34] Many GPEW members saw themselves as analogous to Syriza and Podemos and saw mirroring UKIP as an opportunity to succeed. "The growth of Syriza, Podemos or ourselves partly just reflects a massive disillusionment with politics as usual, business as usual, and wanting alternatives", argues Caroline Lucas, "and the challenge for us in the UK was to demonstrate that that alternative didn't have to be in the backward-looking UKIP, but could be a very positive, upbeat, socially and environmentally-committed party." Natalie Bennett would use her 2015 Party Conference speech to tell the GPEW, "our politics is rotten. Our finance sector is rotten. Our industrial sector is rotten", concluding that "the core is rotten – it must be removed."[35] The success of UKIP and left-wing populists in southern Europe provided an example that would, to an extent, be employed by the Greens.

From 2005 onwards, Britain's three mainstream parties put forward increasingly anti-immigration and anti-multiculturalist messages in response to the growing public unease over unprecedented immigration levels. The resulting growth of UKIP, in particular, changed both the terms of debate and the tone of British politics, as well as reflecting an emerging pan-European cultural divide over the issue of national homogeneity. As the Conservatives, Labour and the Liberal Democrats responded in a more sympathetic manner to UKIP's message, voters with the most pro-immigration and pro-multiculturalist sentiments, characterised as 'libertarian-universalists', found themselves increasingly distant from the rhetoric of the major parties. Simultaneously, left-wing parties in other parts of Europe successfully fused their anti-austerity rhetoric with the classically populist dichotomy of a pure people and a corrupt elite in order to discredit establishment parties. By 2014, just as there was an occupied space for an anti-establishment, anti-austerity party, there was also an unsatisfied demand for a pro-immigration party, as well as a populistic rhetorical formula that minor parties could use. Moreover, the growth of UKIP left the media hungry for similar stories of insurgent parties undermining the British party system and adding to the unpredictability of the upcoming general election.

Notes

1. Available at: https://www.youtube.com/watch?v=ziZOQ-_NRJo.
2. Thatcher, M. (1989), 'Speech to the United Nations General Assembly (Global Environment)', accessed at http://www.margaretthatcher.org/document/107817 on 20/1/2016.
3. Sommers, J. (2015), 'Nigel Farage Reveals He Voted Green in the 1989 European Parliament Elections', accessed at http://www.huffingtonpost.co.uk/2015/01/25/nigel-farage-green_n_6541610.html on 18/01/2016.
4. Vidal, J. (2015), 'EU car pollution laws have improved UK's air quality, say carmakers', accessed at http://www.theguardian.com/environment/2015/sep/04/eu-car-pollution-laws-have-improved-uks-air-quality-say-carmakers on 20/01/2016.

5. Green Party (2001), Green Party Manifesto: Reach for the Future, accessedathttps://www.greenparty.org.uk/files/reports/2004/2001%20 General%20Election%20manifesto.pdf on 28 April 2016.
6. Pearson-Jones, B. (2015), 'An Interview with Natalie Bennett, accessed at https://www.wessexscene.co.uk/politics/2015/04/30/an-interview-with-natalie-bennett/ on 20/01/2016; Jones, O. (2015), 'Labour "never challenged the austerity narrative"' accessed at https://www.youtube.com/watch?v=iFG3INb7VWU on 20/01/2016
7. Shaheen, Salman (2013), 'Comment: Greens solidify their reputation as the only real alternative to Labour', accessed at http://leftfootforward.org/2013/02/greens-prove-they-are-an-alternative-to-labour/ on 20/01/2016.
8. Green Party Members' Website (2015), 'Has the Green Party Been Hijacked By the Far Left', accessed at https://my.greenparty.org.uk/forum/national-forums/general-member-discussion/8784 on 28/04/2016.
9. BBC News (2013), '2013 council elections: Green Party launches campaign', accessed at http://www.bbc.com/news/uk-politics-22214545 on 28/01/2016
10. HM Government (2010), The Coalition: Our Programme for Government, London, Cabinet Office, pp. 30.
11. Chorley, M. (2014), "Miliband is praying the economy doesn't recover": Clegg pins blame on last Labour government for the cost of living crisis', accessed at http://www.dailymail.co.uk/news/article-2598992/Miliband-praying-economy-doesnt-recover-Clegg-hits-blame-Labour-government-cost-living-crisis.html on 28/04/2016.
12. BBC Points West (2015), 'Bristol Green Surge', accessed at https://www.youtube.com/watch?v=w6UOHVaJerE on 16/01/2016.
13. Robinson, N. (2014), 'Clegg – A very botched coup', accessed at http://www.bbc.co.uk/news/uk-politics-27611002 on 16/01/2016.
14. The full breakdown of February 2014 vote intention of 2015 Green voters is: Green Party: 28 %, Labour: 25 %, Don't Know: 21 %, Liberal Democrats: 11 %, UKIP: 6 %, Would Not Vote: 4 %, Other: 5 %.
15. The full breakdown of 2015 vote choice of those intending to vote Green in February 2014 is: Green Party: 55 %, Labour: 24 %, Liberal Democrats: 8 %, Conservative 6 %.
16. BBC News, 'Tougher climate target unveiled' accessed at http://news.bbc.co.uk/1/hi/uk_politics/7673748.stm on 11/1/16 at 22:50.
17. Tuxworth, B. (2010), 'Will Ed Miliband take Britain's Labor Party from red to green?' accessed at http://grist.org/article/2010-09-29-will-ed-miliband-take-britains-labor-party-from-red-to-green/ on 14/01/2016.

18. The Independent (2011), 'Ed Miliband: Rallying call to 'lost' Lib Dem supporters', accessed at http://www.independent.co.uk/news/people/profiles/ed-miliband-rallying-call-to-lost-lib-dem-supporters-2194477.html on 14/1/2016.
19. Porter, A. & Winnett, R. (2010), 'Ed Miliband: New Labour is dead', accessed at http://www.telegraph.co.uk/news/politics/labour/8026708/Ed-Miliband-New-Labour-is-dead.html on 16/01/2016.
20. Conservative Home (2008), 'Labour has maxed out Britain's credit card, says Cameron', accessed at http://conservativehome.blogs.com/torydiary/2008/11/labour-has-maxe.html on 16/01/2016.
21. Labour Party, 'Labour's Zero-Based Review', accessed at http://www.yourbritain.org.uk/uploads/editor/files/Zero_Based_Review.pdf on 12/1/2016.
22. BBC News, 'Miliband shifts immigration policy, saying Labour 'got it wrong'.' Accessed at http://www.bbc.co.uk/news/uk-politics-18539472 on 12/1/2016.
23. The Guardian (2004), 'Full Text: Blair's climate change speech' accessed at http://www.theguardian.com/politics/2004/sep/15/greenpolitics.uk on 12/1/2016.
24. The Liberal Democrats (2005), 'Liberal Democrats: The REAL Alternative', accessed at http://ucrel.lancs.ac.uk/wmatrix/tutorial/libdem%20manifesto%202005.pdf on 12/1/2016.
25. The Telegraph (2013), 'Now David Cameron really is the heir to Blair', accessed at http://blogs.telegraph.co.uk/news/benedictbrogan/100239329/now-david-cameron-really-is-the-heir-to-blair/ on 12/1/2015.
26. Alibhai-Brown, Y. (1998), 'Let us now praise the surprising successes of multicultural Britain' accessed at http://www.independent.co.uk/voices/let-us-now-praise-the-surprising-successes-of-multicultural-britain-1162441.html on 14/01/2016.
27. The Telegraph (2011), 'Nicolas Sarkozy declares multiculturalism has failed' accessed at http://www.telegraph.co.uk/news/worldnews/europe/france/8317497/Nicolas-Sarkozy-declares-multiculturalism-had-failed.html on 14/01/2016.
28. Eaten, G. (2014), 'Cooper and Lammy's condemnation of Farage as "racist" puts pressure on Miliband', accessed at http://www.newstatesman.com/politics/2014/05/cooper-and-lammys-condemnation-farage-racist-puts-pressure-miliband on 13/01/2016.
29. 2014-2017 British Election Study Panel Survey accessed at http://www.britishelectionstudy.com/data-objects/panel-study-data/ on 12/1/2016, all calculations exclude 'Don't Knows'.

30. Data taken from Google Trends, accessed at https://www.google.co.uk/trends/ on 13/1/2016.
31. Goodwin, M. & Ford, R. (2013), 'Just how much media coverage does UKIP get?', accessed at http://www.newstatesman.com/politics/2013/11/just-how-much-media-coverage-does-ukip-get on 13/1/2016.
32. Bennhold, K. (2015), 'UKIP Has Changed Britain's Conversation. Now It Needs a Big Win', accessed at http://www.nytimes.com/2015/05/02/world/europe/ukip-has-changed-britains-conversation-now-it-needs-a-big-win.html?_r=0 on 14/1/2016.
33. Hope, C. (2015) 'Nigel Farage: I hope future generations are proud of me when I am 'dead and gone'', accessed at http://www.telegraph.co.uk/news/politics/nigel-farage/11590225/Nigel-Farage-I-hope-future-generations-are-proud-of-me-when-I-am-dead-and-gone.html on 16/01/2016.
34. Mudde, C. (2015), 'The problem with populism', accessed at http://www.theguardian.com/commentisfree/2015/feb/17/problem-populism-syriza-podemos-dark-side-europe on 16/01/2016.
35. Bennett, N. (2015), 'Full Speech: Natalie Bennett addresses Green Party Autumn Conference in Bournemouth', accessed at https://www.greenparty.org.uk/news/2015/09/25/full-speech-natalie-bennett-addresses-green-party-autumn-conference-in-bournemouth/ on 16/01/2016.

Bibliography

Bornschier, S. (2010), *Cleavage politics and the populist right: the new cultural conflict in Western Europe*. Philadelphia: Temple University Press

Bornschier, S. and Kriesi, H. (2012), 'The populist right, the working class, and the changing face of class politics' in *Class Politics and the Radical Right* (ed. Rydgren, J.). Oxford: Routledge, 10–30

Burchell, J. (2002), *The Evolution of Green Politics: Development & Change within European Green Parties*, London: Earthscan

Capra, F. and Spretnak, C. (1984), *The Global Promise of Green Politics*, New York: E. P. Dutton.

Cowley, P. and Kavanagh, D. (2015), *The British General Election of 2015*, Basingstoke: Palgrave Macmillan

Cutts, D. and Russell, A. (2015), 'From Coalition to Catastrophe: The Electoral Meltdown of the Liberal Democrats' in *Parliamentary Affairs* 68, (suppl 1), 70–87

Dennison, J. (2015), 'The Other Insurgency? The Greens and the Election' in *Parliamentary Affairs*, 68 (suppl 1), 188–205

Dennison, J. and Goodwin, M. (2015), 'Immigration, Issue Ownership and the Rise of UKIP' in *Parliamentary Affairs*, 68 (suppl 1), 168–187

Fielding, S. (2015), "Hell, No!' Labour's Campaign: The Correct Diagnosis but the Wrong Doctor?' in *Parliamentary Affairs*, 68 (suppl 1), 54–69
Fieldhouse, E., J. Green., G. Evans., H. Schmitt, C. van der Eijk, J. Mellon & C. Prosser (2016), British Election Study Internet Panel Waves 1–9
Gamble, A. (2015), 'The Economy' in *Parliamentary Affairs* 68 (suppl 1), 154–167
Goodwin, M. and Milazzo, C. (2015), *UKIP: Inside the Campaign to Redraw the Map of British Politics*, Oxford: Oxford University Press
Hazell, R. and Yong, B. (2012), *The Politics of Coalition*, Oxford: Hart Publishing
Inglehart, R. (1971) 'The Silent Revolution in Europe: Intergenerational Change in Post-industrial Societies' in American Political Science Review, 65 (December): 991–1017
Kriesi, H., Grande, E., Lachat, R., Dolezal, M., Bornschier, S. and Frey, T. (2008), *West European Politics in the Age of Globalisation*, Cambridge: Cambridge University Press
Mudde, C. (2004), 'The Populist Zeitgeist' in *Government and Opposition*, 39(4), 542–563
Nehring, H. (2008), 'Great Britain' in eds. Klimke, M. and Scharloth, J., *1968: A History of Protest and Activism, 1956–1977.* New York: Palgrave Macmillan, 125–136
Richardson, D. and Rootes, C. (eds) (1995) *The Green Challenge: The Development of Green Parties in Europe.* London: Routledge
Whiteley, P.F. and Sanders, D., British Election Study, 2010: Face-to-Face Survey [computer file]. Colchester, Essex: UK Data Archive [distributor], August 2014

CHAPTER 3

'Green Spike': European Elections to Independence Referendum

Abstract In this chapter, I show how the 2014 European elections and local elections created an opportunity for voters to switch their General Election vote intention to the Greens, resulting in a sudden upturn in the party's poll ratings. This upturn in the Greens' poll ratings was entirely consistent, albeit from a slightly higher baseline, with trends from previous European elections, demonstrating a clear spillover effect. However, along with an improved return of seats in both European and local elections, the Greens' higher poll ratings set the scene for enthusiastic party coverage throughout the summer by media keen for a second UKIP-esque insurgency narrative. During this period, key organisational and personnel changes in the party, typical of 'professionalising' Green parties across Europe, improved the Green Party's ability to exploit the greater membership and media coverage that would soon follow, as well as re-exposing rifts within the party. North of the border, the Scottish Greens quintupled their membership in the week following the Scottish independence referendum as environmentalist, left-libertarian and less sentimentally nationalistic pro-independence Scots were attracted to the Greens as an alternative to the SNP.

Keywords Green Party • Scottish Greens • European elections • Professionalisation • Independence referendum • Party membership • Scottish National Party

J. Dennison, *The Greens in British Politics*,
DOI 10.1007/978-3-319-42673-0_3

2014 European and Local Elections

The GPEW went into 2014 with low expectations, with general election polls putting the party at between two and three per cent. The poor polling followed a series of disappointing local elections results between 2010 and 2013, with the Greens winning just 3.5 per cent of the vote each year, almost half of their 2009 figure. More pressingly, the Greens were set to see their vote share at the 2014 European elections plummet as polls consistently put the Greens at around five per cent, well below their 2009 result of 8.6 per cent. Despite publicly proclaiming an ambition to increase their MEPs from two to six, in private the party was far more concerned with retaining its existing two seats.[1] Chris Luffingham, National Campaigns Director, admits that, based on the polling, "we never thought we were going to get anywhere near [… six seats …] we were going to return no MEPs." Upon taking up his new role in early 2014, Tom Beckett, GPEW Operations and Fundraising Director, was told, "we expect to lose one MEP and we're on track to lose Caroline Lucas in 2015."[2]

The prospect of a poor European performance particularly alarmed the Greens because of their relatively strong record of representation in the European Parliament, voting motivations for which tend to favour Green parties. Our understanding of voting in European elections has been dominated by Reif and Schmitt's (1980) second-order thesis, which posits that "low salience" European Parliament elections are actually fought with "a focus on the national arena" rather than politics within the European institutions (Hix and Marsh 2011: 5). This unique electoral dynamic of European elections is supposed to lead to (1) increased anti-incumbent voting (Heath et al. 1999), (2) protest voting to express dissatisfaction with the mainstream parties generally (Ford et al. 2012), (3) more sincere voting and, subsequently, increased voting for smaller parties and (4) increased voting on issues that voters particularly care about, such as environment or immigration policies.

However, the Greens' ability to attract voters via sincere voting or single-issue voting was undermined by the public's perception of the party as a single-issue environmentalist outfit in a political context dominated by the topics of austerity and immigration. Moreover, environmentalist attitudes had been declining in the UK since at least the mid 2000s. Whereas, in 2006, Britons were almost as likely to agree that "car users should pay higher taxes for the sake of the environment" as to believe that "people should be allowed to use their cars as much as they like even if it damages the environment", by 2014, respondents were nearly twice as likely to believe the latter (Source: British Social Attitudes Survey). Despite record flooding in January and February 2014, which was blamed on climate change by 47 per cent of Britons, the Greens' poll ratings did not change. In March, the environment was rated as one of the top three most important issues by just eleven per cent of the population – behind the economy, immigration, health, housing, Europe, pensions and education.[3, 4]

The low salience of environmentalism was coupled with a low media interest in the Greens. The proportion of newspaper articles referring to the GPEW–as a percentage of those referring to any of the five major English parties–remained low at around only five per cent in January 2014 (Source: LexisNexis). In contrast, UKIP dominated media coverage and were the obvious choice for voters disgruntled with mainstream parties (Goodwin and Milazzo 2015). One member of the Young Greens commented that "the BBC seemed to be largely ignoring the Green Party altogether, preferring to focus on fuelling the hysteria around UKIP, at times appearing to run UKIP's campaign for them."[5]

The GPEW launched its European manifesto on 10 April to little fanfare. Despite their public image as a single-issue party, the Greens' platform gave priority to economic issues in light of the financial crisis and included policies such as introducing a financial transactions tax, capping bankers' bonuses and regulating credit ratings agencies. One of the manifesto's co-authors, Brian Heatley, would later express regret over how far the party consciously downplayed its environmentalist policies, such as cutting EU greenhouse gas emissions by 90 per cent, in 2014.

Moreover, while campaigning the Greens concluded that a mix of leftist economics, often framed as anti-austerity, combined with anti-UKIP rhetoric, was their most potent messaging strategy. Natalie Bennett claimed that the most effective "crowd-pleasers" at public meetings were "rail renationalisation, removing the profit motive from the NHS and ending student tuition fees."[6] She also contrasted her party's message of "hope" with both UKIP's message of "fear" and the "race to the bottom rhetoric" on immigration of all of the mainstream parties.

Prior to the 2014 elections, Green campaigners employed similar tactics. Adam Ramsay, a long-time Green campaigner and a former editor of the website Bright Green, remembers that "campaigning in Oxford we had two main messages." The first of these was to "say to students [...] if you want to make absolutely clear that this patch of Oxford tells UKIP to f--k off, you can vote Green." By contrast, "for old council housing" the Oxford Greens campaigned on an anti-austerity message by "listing the things the Tory council was cutting, particularly adult care services" and then demonstrating that Labour were not proposing to reverse these cuts. The European campaign's anti-UKIP and anti-austerity dual message would often be deployed again one year later at the general election.

The Greens' campaign in the South West region was a notable exception to the party's twin-messaging strategy. The Greens' ultimately successful candidate there, Molly Scott Cato, ran a campaign that focused entirely on wooing former Liberal Democrats. Her campaign manager advised her to not "think about anything except winning the Lib Dem base." Scott Cato contrasts her approach with that of other Greens who refused to target certain types of voters for fear of putting others off "because they say 'well, everybody *might* vote Green.'" Molly Scott Cato concluded that targeting former Liberal Democrats precluded an overly negative campaign of anti-austerity and anti-UKIP messaging: "Lib Dem voters are very similar to Green voters in their concerns, but, if I can summarise this in a nice way, they're very wet. So if you're anti-austerity, anti-anything, knocking anybody, they get really upset about it." Instead, the Greens' campaign in the South West focussed on the economic potential of the region, particularly through increased use of renewable energy, Common Agricultural Policy (CAP) reform and renationalising the railways, as well as reassuring would-be tactical voters that the Greens had a realistic chance of winning a seat.

During the final month before the European elections, the Greens experienced a sudden, late upsurge in polling. Around this time one poll placed the Greens as the third most popular choice for students, and by the beginning of May some polls were putting the Greens ahead of the Liberal Democrats.[7] While leader Natalie Bennett interpreted this late uptick as evidence that her anti-austerity and anti-UKIP messaging strategy was working, an almost identical late increase in support had happened five years earlier at the 2009 European election (see Fig. 3.1).[8] The late uptick in Green support prior to *both* European elections suggests that the Greens only enter the voters' consciousness as a suitable anti-incumbent, protest, sincere or single-issue electoral choice as election day nears and the nature of the elections–proportional and 'second-order'–dawns on the electorate.

At the election, on 22 May, the combined vote share of the GPEW and Scottish Greens was just seven per cent–down from their eight per cent five years earlier. In spite of this decline, the GPEW finished ahead of the Liberal Democrats, giving them fourth place in terms of vote share, their highest

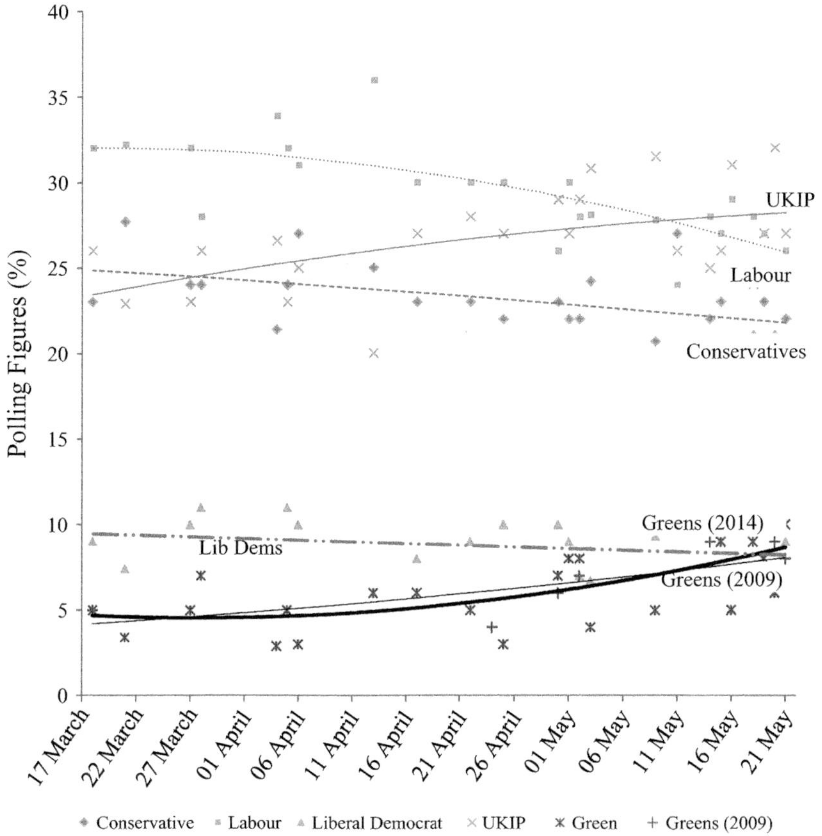

Fig. 3.1 Polling for the 2014 European Parliament elections and, for the Green Party, the 2009 European Election (The dates of the 2009 European elections are realigned to coincide with the days prior to the election in 2014) (Source: UK Polling Report)

position since 1994. The GPEW also won an additional, third MEP, Molly Scott Cato, in the South West, which, alongside Scotland, was one of only two of Britain's twelve regions that saw an increase in the Greens' vote. "The brief for the Euro elections was 'don't screw up, don't lose an MEP'", remembers GPEW Management Coordinator Mark Cridge, "getting Molly was a total surprise." Despite their vote share falling by a percentage point, the Greens were able to present the European elections as a success.

The simultaneous 2014 local elections in parts of England added to the sense of success, in this case more unequivocally. The GPEW gained 18 seats and increased its vote share to 6.6 per cent from 3.5 per cent in the previous year, while the party became the official opposition in traditionally Labour areas such as Liverpool, Solihull, Islington, Norwich and Lewisham. [9] The Greens also secured more than 45 per cent of the vote in two seats in Bristol, highlighting the city as a tantalisingly possible source of a second Westminster seat.

Despite their falling European vote share, the media and GPEW used the party's fourth-place finish and improved local performance to begin framing the Greens as a potential threat to Labour's electoral strategy of relying on disaffected Liberal Democrats.[10] Furthermore, the proportion of newspaper articles referring to the Greens, as a percentage of those mentioning any of the five English parties, increased steadily from 5.6 per cent at the beginning of March to 8.2 per cent by June (Source: LexisNexis). Simultaneously, the party's *general election* poll ratings increased around the time of the European election (see Fig. 3.2).

A spike in general election vote intention for the Greens around the time of the European elections occurred during each of the last three election cycles. In both 2004 and 2009, the Greens' general election polling figures doubled in the months prior to the European election, only to gradually decline throughout the following summer. However, the base from which the Greens' polling spike occurred was progressively higher in each of the three electoral cycles so that, whereas the Greens' polling peaked at around three per cent in 2004, ten years later the peak was around five per cent, suggestive of a steady increase in the fundamental support for the Greens over the last decade. Only 27 per cent of those who switched their general election vote intention to the Greens between March and June of 2014 actually voted Green in May 2015 (British Election Study 2014–2017). However, this was a substantially larger number of voters, in real terms, than in previous elections.

How can we explain the Greens' regular uptick in general election polls around the time of the European elections? The Greens' relatively higher prominence, and thus importance, in European elections incentivises unusually high media coverage, providing the party with the "oxygen of publicity" (Franklin and Curtice 1996) and reducing information costs for voters, thus lowering the electorate's uncertainty about the party (Kroh et al. 2007: 221). This effect is likely to have been particularly strong throughout the last three electoral cycles because, unlike prior

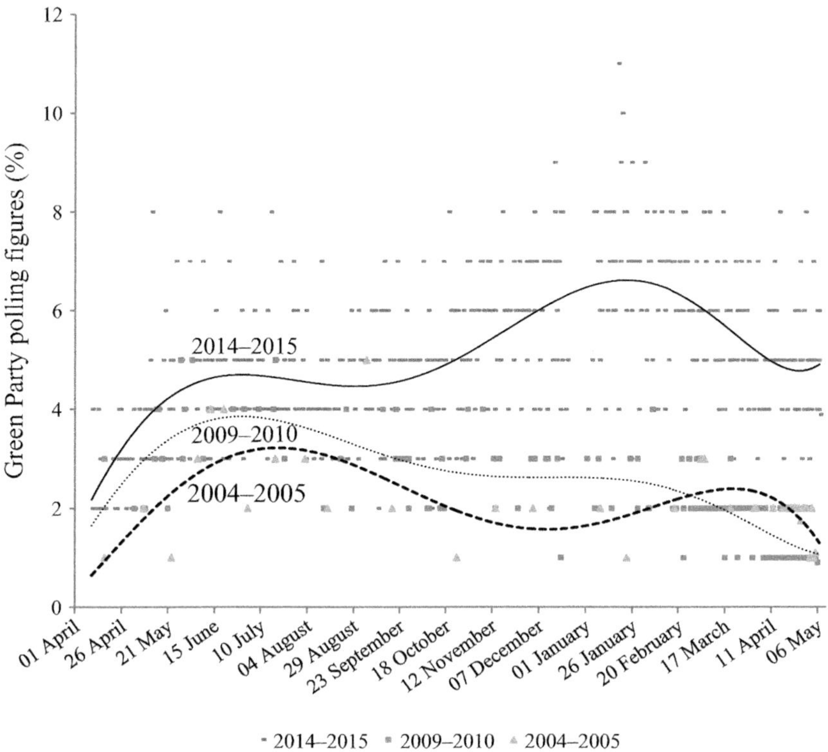

Fig. 3.2 Green Party polling for the 2005, 2010 and 2015 General Elections (Source: UK Polling Report)

to 2004, each of these European elections was held just one year before the national election, meaning that there was less time for the effect to fade. Furthermore, European elections held prior to national elections are treated by parties, the media and voters as "marker-setting elections" for the upcoming 'first order' election and thus of greater significance than those held after the domestic contest (van der Eijk et al. 1996: 301). However, whereas this effect faded over the summers following the European elections in both of the previous electoral cycles, in 2014, the Greens' general election poll ratings remained stable. The party's radical stance on the left-right spectrum, encapsulated and given relevance through its opposition to austerity, increased its domestic newsworthiness

(Bale 2012). This was underscored in the voters' minds as the Greens continued campaigning on identical domestic issues both before and after the European elections, reducing information costs for voters who were confronted with continuous and consistent messaging.

The Greens had entered 2014 fearful of a wipe-out in the European and local elections and, indeed, their European vote share did fall. However, following a typically late surge in support, the party won an additional MEP in the South West, the only region where the GPEW's vote share increased. This late increase in polling was interpreted by the Greens as support for its anti-austerity and anti-UKIP messaging, though in reality the Greens' polling in the run-up to the election was nearly identical to what it had been in 2009 and the party's best performance was in the South West, where its anti-austerity and anti-UKIP message was mostly absent. The anti-austerity messaging, however, did offer the Greens' relevance to the upcoming domestic contest and may partially explain their far greater ability to retain prospective voters after the European elections in 2014 than previously. The narrative that the Greens and the increasingly interested media put forward was of a party with 50 per cent more MEPs that finished ahead of the governing Liberal Democrats–arguably their natural rivals for voters–and with a growing presence in local government. Inside the party, fear of an abysmal performance gave way to relief, which would soon, with media backing, become expectations of greater things to come.

Organisational Change: Amateur-activists to Professional-Electoralists?

In late 2013, the GPEW, wary of electoral setbacks over the following year and a half, accelerated internal organisational changes, building upon the operational and strategic transformation of the party over the past half-decade. The GPEW's 'professionalisation' was hardly out of the ordinary. Rihoux and Frankland (2008) show that most Green parties in advanced democracies have, to varying extents and with distinctive national caveats, transformed from 'amateur-activists' to 'professional-electoralists'. This transformation, in organisational terms, sees a centralisation of power away from local parties and activists towards an increasingly personal and less collective leadership surrounded by a professional staff. In this sense, the Greens across Europe and beyond have been willing to sacrifice a degree of their direct-democratic, decentralising ideology, in exchange for increased political power, often against the wishes of segments of their membership. However, the transformation of the European Green parties remains partial, leading Rihoux and Frankland to compare them to "'centaurs', with professional-electoral, efficiency-seeking heads, but still amateur-activist, participation-seeking bodies" (2008: 284).

Of all of the Green parties that Rihoux and Frankland considered, the GPEW had, in 2008, made the least progress along this professionalising trajectory, perhaps even moving backwards. The party's movement towards 'professional-electoralism' had partially been impeded by, at times, damaging in-fighting. Rüdig (2008: 199, 216) argues that the party's "key internal divide, between the so-called 'electoralists' and 'anarchists', centred on the question of how the party should be internally structured. Despite this, there have been few significant changes of party structure over the years: there has been much more continuity than change." The GPEW started out less 'amateur-activist' than its European sister parties but, by the mid-2000s, had been overtaken in terms of professionalisation.

This divide re-emerged most clearly in 2007, with the party split over whether it should continue with its two 'Principal Speakers' leadership model, or adopt a more election-focussed single leader model. Though one Green Member of the London Assembly called the prospective change "a naive and forlorn hope", the electoralists, led by Caroline Lucas, emerged triumphant.[11] Following the party's subsequent Brighton Pavilion victory in 2010, the momentum in the party moved sharply to the electoralists, though not without on-going objections from more ideologically minded Greens. Throughout the 2010–2015 Parliament, and particularly after the 2014 European elections, the Greens overhauled their membership systems, digital and communications strategy, staff, donations strategy and regional structures. Burchell (2002) argues in his comparative study of the German, French, Swedish and British Greens that organisational change occurs in political parties after a change of leadership, a change of the ruling faction in a party or an external event such as a particularly good or particularly bad election. For the Greens, the motivation for continued change was rooted in the particularly good result of gaining an MP in 2010, the fear of losing that seat in 2015 and, amongst more ambitious members, out of hope that they might increase their electoral support.

Mark Cridge, former Management Coordinator on GPEx and a marketing entrepreneur, took responsibility for transforming the party's membership system and digital strategy during his 2011–2015 term. "Whenever you're in a voluntary organisation … inevitably things are not well documented from a digital perspective … it was a horrific mess. Next year and a half we spent putting infrastructure and platforms in place, so we upgraded … the membership system, even though we thought we had 13,000 members, only 8,500 were giving us any money … we put in place the digital strategy – very importantly we recognised that the golden rule was to gather information centrally in a common format. … We put in [a system] so that members of the public could go from knowing nothing to being deemed a 'supporter', which was 'give me your email address and you'll hear about us' to moving on to becoming a volunteer to becoming a member. … The Green Surge was made possible because of the infrastructure." Changes to the membership systems, including easing and graduating the process of becoming a member, would later facilitate the 2014–2015 'Surge' in membership, the party's resulting inflated budget and its ability to place candidates in far more seats than ever before.

The GPEW's two new directors–both full-time professional staff–Chris Luffingham, National Campaigns Director, and Tom Beckett, Director of Fundraising and Operations, took their positions in early February 2014. The directors overhauled much of the GPEW's communications and fundraising capabilities. Though the most sweeping changes happened after the European elections, important communications strategies were immediately employed such as revamped newsletters to members, setting up of a phone bank for enquiries from the public and the use of social media activists, which would be widely employed over the summer. Tom Beckett states, "we got 500 social media activists who signed up during the European elections who tweeted on particular issues or sent Facebook messages on particular issues. We had drives on particular issues, Chris developed a messaging calendar." These social media activists "were all about data capture and using people to deliver particular tasks and make sure you were speaking to the right kind of audience." For a party with just 14,000 members, the GPEW's increase in communications and data collection capability was considerable.

The increasing resonance of the party's message fuelled donations as the European and then general election approached. "On my first day in the office", remembers Chris Luffingham, "Kate the office manager opened an envelope, and I kind of looked around and I said, 'You alright?' She said, 'Yes, we've just had a bequest for £188,000, and this was somebody that wasn't on our membership, we've never had any contact with him, but he had left us a house." The Greens had previously expected to raise just £40,000 for the European campaign. The new income was quickly spent on a policy and communications officer, a digital officer and a fundraising and membership office, as well as putting money aside for Caroline Lucas' 2015 campaign. Another donation of around £18,000 was handed out to regional parties. A full fundraising strategy, with impressive results, would be instigated in late 2014.

Following the European elections, the GPEW underwent far more fundamental changes in its internal operations. By the end of the year, the GPEW had a five-year financial strategy, fundraising campaigns, greater communications and campaigning guidance for local party officers, a redesigned website to allow people to sign up as volunteers and contact their local officer, paperless memberships, and a month-by-month bi-annual budget plan. The directors initiated a new regional tier in the party of Regional Campaigns Coordinators in order to better facilitate communications from the 190 local parties, reduce the troubleshooting burden on the central office and, most importantly, redirect regional funds to the key constituency campaigns, which the coordinators would then help to manage. Over the summer, the party held telephone fundraising campaigns for members, recruiting 2,500 regular donors, and raising a pot of around £110,000 a year to pay for the Regional Campaigns Coordinators. A Green Growth Fund was created with an accompanying strategy to demonstrate to potential major donors the ambitions and objectives of the party. Furthermore, the directors managed to circumvent the annual Green Party Executive Committee elections in the summer, which Green members with a zeal for 'professionalisation' described as "cumbersome", "unhelpful" and "disruptive" to election planning, by having a two-year month-by-month spending plan drawn up, thus taking day-by-day budgetary power away from the party's democratically elected executive and placing it in the hands of professionals over the long-term.

Just as had happened in the early 1990s, such rapid changes in the GPEW ruffled feathers. As one member said, the new directors "put a few noses out of joint." Indeed, accelerated 'professionalisation' in the GPEW exposed three particular rifts within the party: whether decisions should be made centrally by professional staff or democratically by the membership; whether the party should adopt a targeted or decentralised approach to campaigning; and whether the party's primary objective was winning elections or campaigning on issues.

The increasingly centralised control of finances mandated uncomfortable changes for veteran party activists. Tom Beckett himself states, "whether we ran the show? I think, yeah, we wrote the strategy for expenditure, we got all the extra money to go away and make campaigns, and we fundamentally changed the ambition of what the party felt it was able to do. That was backed up by a lot of members who wanted to get on the back of that. To do that, some in the party felt the decisions weren't as democratic as they could have been." Judy Maciejowska, a long-time campaigner, recalls that whereas in previous campaigns she had direct control over spending decisions, "now it'll go to the directors ... as a party we cannot be run purely by volunteers." However, not only did the party's increased central control run contrary to the GPEW's stated aim of a society organised by "voluntary co-operation", but also had some Greens questioning its effectiveness.[12] Matt Hawkins, Media Officer for the London Green Party, argues against professionalisation "because I think that one of the great things actually about our party is that it's built on passion, it's built on volunteers." Shahrar Ali, one of the GPEW's two Deputy Leaders, argues that "if you were to over-professionalise", that would "denude the volunteer force", which is "really where our strength is."

The professionalisation of the party also included the imposition of an electoral strategy that saw electioneering in terms of a strict methodology and disregarded local nuances. As National Campaigns Director, Chris Luffingham took a firm line on imposing a uniform procedure for winning elections. "Local parties like to say, 'We're slightly different. We don't do this and we don't do that. We're not like that constituency over there' ... Actually, yes you are. You have to follow the process. ... Winning elections is not a philosophy, it's not some sort of ideology, it's a science." This mentality would cause serious friction within the party. In the weeks running up to the general election, the Green Party in Bristol West, a target seat, decided to withhold their data from the central party and banned Chris Luffingham from physically entering their constituency, a stance that would be ratified by GPEx only 18 months after originally hiring him.

More controversial still was the party's long-term 'target-to-win' strategy. This electoral approach attempted to overcome the harsh realities of Westminster's majoritarian electoral system by pooling resources from a wide area and using them in the most promising wards, districts and constituencies. Its advocates argued that the added exposure of elected Green politicians made the strategy worthwhile, in the long term, even for those areas that saw their resources funnelled away. As Brian Heatley, co-author of the 2010 and 2015 GPEW manifestos, acknowledges, 'the only way we'll make progress is by getting local councillors and county councillors and gradually covering the constituency … as they did in Brighton … So this might have not pleased our parliamentary candidate but you're only going to do so much campaigning, so you might as well do it all in one place.' Though the strategy was first announced in the mid-1990s, targeting of resources remained a major point of tension within the party. Indeed, GPEW parliamentary candidates rarely had a realistic chance of winning their seat and so often lost out financially to local election priorities via the target-to-win system which reallocated resources not only between constituencies but also within them. As such, many parliamentary candidates were less keen on the approach than officials in the national party. As Vix Lothian, who won an impressive 13.4 per cent of the vote as 2015 GPEW parliamentary candidate for the Isle of Wight, put it, "our entire approach rejected target-to-win."

Target-to-win also prescribed an approach to campaigning that further moved the party away from its Green philosophical roots. The party's main target-to-win briefing advises canvassers to repeatedly refer to the candidate's name and picture, rather than the party's, a move towards personalised campaigns typical of more electoralist parties (Lucardie and Rihoux 2008: 10). [13] Furthermore, the target-to-win strategy included full scripts on how to deal with different types of voters over the phone, devoid of ideology and focused purely on vote maximising. The script recommends reminding would-be Labour voters, "Do you know you have 3 Labour Councillors in this area at the moment, which means they have the monopoly? [Green candidate] has been working all year round – you have probably seen the newsletters – and many Labour people are backing [Green candidate] this time around just so that there is more of a mixture. Two Labour Councillors and [Green candidate] elected would mean that there are checks and balances and each councillor is held to account." Another script says that if the voter supports "BNP or UKIP, then do not tell them that there is no BNP or UKIP candidate (unless they are very anti-Green) but if they appear to be very anti-Labour, then we do want them to go to the polling station. When they get there, they will see no BNP or UKIP candidate and so may vote Green instead." In this sense, the Greens took an electoralists decision to downplay issues and ideology from their campaigns, instead partially promoting themselves in terms of protest and tactical voting.

The GPEW's transformation from 'amateur-activists' to 'professional-electoralists' ran at odds with the prevailing view in sections of the party that its primarily role was not only fighting elections but also fighting single-issue campaigns. Peter Tatchell, journalist and Green Party campaigner, explained in 2007 that 'the Greens are not obsessed with elections and parliament, we are also committed to grassroots direct action protest and community empowerment.'[14] Indeed, even Green MEP Keith Taylor argues that "the function of a Green Party is not running things … our purpose is to point towards the ways in which things should be run, to actually stretch the grounds of terrains to include our agenda." One, more election-minded, Green laments that "there is a school of thought in the Green Party that doesn't even want to be in opposition, they would rather be campaigning against the whole political edifice, characteristic of a movement or campaigning organisation, rather than people who want to get elected and to govern. We're even one stage back. We have tiny numbers of people who actually want to be elected."

Other members, such as Sam Riches, Policy Coordinator for GPEx, found their colleagues' tendency to discuss society's ills, rather than impose solutions via winning elections, to be frustrating. She argues that "there is resistance against professionalisation … the three people and the dog who have been the local party for the past 20 years … would actually quite like to go back to just being a little debating society that meets in the pub once a month … there is a wonderful security about being on the moral high ground and never having to test your principles because it's all the fault of the system." Moving towards a more electorally focused mentality was a prime objective of the party's new National Campaigns Director, Chris Luffingham. "The party's almost split in two. There are quite a few people within the party that in their heart of hearts, would still like to be a kind of campaign pressure group. And it kind of winds me up, actually, because I keep hearing every now and then that there are other ways to affect change other than through winning elections. That's fine and that's true. Go join Greenpeace. Because we are a political party, this is what we do. We win elections, and that's how we affect change."

Overall, in 2014 the GPEW took steps away from being an 'amateur-activist' party and towards a 'professional-electoralist' party, in a similar vein to transformations of many Green parties in advanced democracies since the 1980s. Of these, administrative improvements to the party's membership system and communications and digital strategy were hardly controversial. However, the conscious transfer of decision-making power on long-term budgetary and strategic issues to professional staff in order to override the "destabilising" annual GPEx elections was a more obvious break with the Greens' ideological commitment to internal democracy.

Furthermore, the imposition of a new regional layer of campaigners coupled with the pre-existing 'target-to-win' strategy also contradicted the Green commitment to decentralised power. Whereas Burchell (2002: 122) argued that the GPEW's "apparent division over its 'primary goal' contributed to the bitter conflicts surrounding party organization", by 2014 the 'professional-electoralist' wing of the party was clearly in the driving seat, leaving the 'amateur-activists' to occasionally grumble and protest against an increasingly focused central party and membership.

The Green 'Yes' to Scottish Independence: A Route to a Fairer Society

Since the division of the UK Green Party in 1989, the Scottish Greens have tended to fare worse than the GPEW in European, general and local elections and, instead, have achieved their greatest successes in Scottish Parliament elections. The Scottish Greens have attracted a smaller vote share than their sister party in England and Wales at every general election since 1997[15] and, until 2014, at every European election.[16] Even the considerably more proportional electoral system for Scottish local elections–the Single Transferable Vote–has only given the Scottish Greens slightly better outcomes than their English and Welsh counterparts in terms of winning council seats. The 2012 local elections saw the Scottish Greens win just 14 out of 1223 seats, just over one per cent and not much better than the 0.7 per cent of council seats held by the Greens in England and Wales, which were won in majoritarian contests.

The main reason for the Scottish Greens' relative under-performance has been their far greater electoral competition. Young, well-educated, left-wing voters have had the choice between the historically dominant and, in post-industrial areas, culturally ingrained Labour Party, a particularly strong Liberal Democrat presence and the intermittently significant Scottish Socialist Party (SSP). Moreover, as in Wales, where the GPEW do relatively poorly, the Scottish Greens must also compete with an arguably left-libertarian nationalist party– the Scottish National Party (SNP).

The obvious exception to the Scottish Greens' historic under-performance has been their results in elections to the Scottish Parliament. The party have been able to exploit Holyrood's Additional Member System, which allocates some seats by first-past-the-post and the remainder from regional lists using the d'Hondt method. The Greens have focussed on gaining seats via the latter list vote and, prior to 2016, usually did not even put forward candidates for constituency seats. In doing so, they have retained continuous representation in the legislature since it was established in 1999, when Robin Harper became the first Green parliamentarian in the UK.

In particular, the Scottish Greens secured an impressive electoral result in 2003 by winning seven Members of the Scottish Parliament (MSPs), despite having a headquarters of just two paid staff members and relying on a neighbouring pub for free Wi-Fi.[17] At the party's conference less than two years earlier only 35 members had been present, leading one MSP of 2003–7 to reflect that "if you attended the Scottish Green Party conference in 2001, you had a 20 per cent chance of being an MSP in less than two years."[18] In 2003, a weakened SNP and a Labour Party that had just embarked on the War in Iraq left voters looking for left-wing alternatives. Moreover, perceived similarities between the four major Scottish parties and their erstwhile tendency to ignore potential threats from minor parties aided both the Greens and the SSP, who also won six seats.[19] The Scottish Greens' campaign toned down the usual environmentalism and focused singularly on reminding voters to 'Second Vote Green', referring to the regional list vote, in an age before other Scottish parties had fully appreciated the nuances of their recently created electoral system.

Though the Greens celebrated winning their seven seats, commentators (e.g. Burnside et al. 2003: 12) immediately warned that the party's success, based on just seven per cent of the vote, was fragile and reliant on voters' estimation of the election as unimportant. Indeed, the following Scottish Parliament elections in 2007 saw the number of Green MSPs reduced to two, while the SSP was wiped out following a high-profile internal scandal. By 2011, the Scottish Greens were the only 'minor' Scottish party capable of securing representation in the Scottish Parliament, even if this was based on just 4.4 per cent of the regional list vote and zero per cent of the constituency vote.

From October 2012, when the Edinburgh Agreement for a referendum on Scottish independence was signed, the media increasingly framed the Scottish Greens as one of two major pro-independence parties, boosting their public profile. The party leadership initially pulled out of the main pro-independence campaign group–'Yes Scotland'–criticising the dominant role that the SNP played in the organisation and lamenting its pledges to retain the monarchy, pound sterling and membership of NATO as a "strategy for failure."[20] At the party's 2012 conference, the 100 or so Green members attending, with the leadership's backing, voted to overturn the decision. Though some delegates feared the "embrace of the SNP" in the campaign and rallied against SNP leader Alex Salmond's vision for an independent Scotland, a majority present agreed that the party would be ignored if they did not join the 'Yes' Campaign.[21] To reaffirm their commitment to radicalism, the Greens also joined the Radical Independence Campaign (RIC), which championed an alternative vision of an independent Scotland as a "society of equality", with "a great welfare state" and "a just economy", thus underlining their more left-wing, anti-establishment outlook.[22] The RIC's message focussed on anti-austerity and the primarily Conservative nature of the UK government and emphasised that "Britain is for the rich, Scotland can be ours."[23] The Greens went into the referendum campaign benefitting from the profile of the mainstream 'Yes Scotland' organisation but, via membership of other organisations as well as their own campaigning, retained a distinctive voice.

If "the Scottish Question had never been about national identity, nor constitutional status but was about the kind of state and society people envisaged" (Mitchell 2015: 90) then the Greens' answer was unequivocally distinct from the low corporation tax, North Sea oil-driven economic model put forward by the SNP. In early 2013 the Greens commissioned a poll that asked, "How much do you agree or disagree with the following statement? In reaching my decision about whether to support Scottish independence, the prospect of a fairer and more equal society is more important to me than whether Scotland as a whole would be slightly richer or slightly poorer."[24] Definitively, 58 per cent agreed and only 10 per cent disagreed. The Greens' radical alternative vision of independence was emphasised in October 2013 when the 'Green Yes' campaign was launched. The party used the launch to convey that they were not nationalist but believed that independence was the only way to deliver the radical change that they desired. Patrick Harvie, the more prominent of the party's two Co-Convenors, framed his argument for independence as not nationalist but progressive and, in fact, beneficial to all four nations of the UK: "for me, it's got nothing to do with flags, or 300 years of history; it's about the future. And I think that the best way, not only of changing Scotland, but actually challenging the nature of UK politics and the way that it works at present, throughout these islands, is Scottish independence."[25] Natalie Bennett, GPEW leader, echoed this view from London.[26]

Harvie framed the need for independence primarily in terms of greater social justice and redistribution of wealth, which he argued the Westminster elite precluded. "The hollowing out of the UK economy by corporate interests, with the main Westminster parties encouraging this approach" meant "satisfying, secure jobs with good pay are increasingly rare."[27] An independent Scotland, on the other hand, "would chart a different course. We could prioritise the small firms that provide us with a stable business base, reform bank lending and put an end to poverty pay."[28] Explicitly, in the final leaders' debate prior to the referendum, Harvie distinguished his position from that of the SNP, stating, "I'm not a nationalist, I'm not driven by feelings of Scottishness or Britishness ... Let's look at the Scotland we have been given. Let's look at the inequality we are left with after years of an economic model that exploits people and the natural ecological resources of our country."[29]

Patrick Harvie managed to increase both his profile and his personal popularity as the referendum campaign continued. His satisfaction ratings increased from 22 per cent in 2010, to 34 per cent in early August of 2014, just prior to the referendum, to 45 per cent in late October, after the referendum.[30] Interestingly, his dissatisfaction rating during that entire period barely moved, staying steady at around 20 per cent. With more exposure, the Greens' leader became a recognised and popular political personality throughout Scotland.

The referendum result–55 per cent against independence and 45 per cent in favour, with an extraordinary turnout of 85 per cent–disappointed many Greens. Andy Collins, Green councillor for North East Fife, described the day after the results as "a day of mourning in Scotland." However, the coming weeks saw a completely unexpected outpouring of support for the pro-independence parties. On the night after the referendum, the Greens tweeted that "since yesterday morning, we've gained 1200 new members. At one point folks were signing up one every 15 seconds."[31] The next afternoon the party exclaimed, "As of 4pm today, we've added 2000 new members. Yeah, I said 2,000! Welcome, all!"[32] Nina Baker, a Green in the Glasgow City Council, remembers how the party was largely unprepared for the membership surge: "It picked up a little bit after the European election. I might be guessing four or five a week, but still completely within manageable bounds. I don't know at the national level, whether we really expected what then happened to us on the day of the referendum ... suddenly there was this torrent coming into the headquarters. I say headquarters, it was an office with one and a bit paid members of staff running the entire Scottish Green party and everything else was done at home by people on a voluntary basis, including the membership secretary."

On 12 October 2014, less than a month after the referendum, the Scottish Greens had over 7,000 members, over four times larger than their pre-referendum total, and by the general election it was 9,000. During the same period the memberships of other Scottish parties also increased, primarily the other pro-independence parties. The SNP's membership rose from around 25,000 to 105,000 and the SSP's membership rose from 1,500 to 3,500. However, the Scottish Greens' growth in members was proportionally the largest by some distance.

How can we explain this membership surge? Given that the pro-independence parties saw increases in their memberships immediately after the referendum, it seems likely that new Green members were pro-independence and motivated by events surrounding the vote. In a classic work on the motivations for party membership, Clark and Wilson (1961) distinguish between three types of incentives–material incentives, such as elected office, business contracts or employment; the social benefits of belonging to an organisation; and the purposive incentives of aiding a cause. Bennie (2004: 206) offered a comprehensive account of the Scottish Greens' membership history from the late 1980s onwards, showing that the motivations were clearly purposive. She shows that "of all the reasons for joining, the members were most likely to agree with the statement, 'the party provides the best opportunity to achieve the political aims I support.'" Bennie goes on to argue that these aims were not limited to the achievement of political goals on particular issues but that "members show every sign of *being committed to a common cause.*" As for when members joined, with some foresight, Bennie (2004: 208) emphasises above all the importance of political context and states that "we can identify periods of 'insurgency' when the political environment dictates" becoming a party member. It seems highly likely that the motivation to join the Scottish Greens in the weeks after the referendum was a purposive commitment to pursuing Scottish independence.

However, the key puzzle remains why some 'Yes'-voting Scots chose to join the Greens rather than the SNP, the obvious pro-independence party. Though data on the membership of the Scottish Greens is not currently available, there is data on pro-independence voters who, just after the referendum, were *intending to vote* for the Greens or the SNP at the next Scottish Parliament election, which can be used, with caution, as a proxy for data on the profiles of each party's new members. Fig. 3.3 shows the social and ideological profiles of pro-independence Green supporters in the aftermath of the referendum compared to pro-independence supporters of the SNP and the Scottish electorate as a whole. The source of this data is the 2014–2017 British Election Study, details of which are provided in Chap. 6.

	SG	SNP	Electorate
Socio Demographics			
Mean age	39	47	47
% under 25	25	11	12
% Male	58	52	48
% White	94	96	97
% University Degree	44	24	28
% Homeowner	47	54	59
% Students	11	5	6
% No Religion	71	55	52
% Higher professional / Management	22	12	15
% Lower professional / Intermediate	58	37	51
% Small employer / Supervisory	10	14	14
% Routine / Semi-Routine	10	28	21
Mean Household Income	26	26	27
Attitudes (1-5 unless otherwise stated: 1=disagree; 3=neither; 5 agree)			
Left-right self placement (0-10)	2.3	3.7	4.4
Govt should redistribute incomes	4.2	4.0	3.7
Public spending cuts too far	4.4	4.2	3.9
Environmental protection too far	1.7	2.4	2.6
Lib-Authoritarian index (0-20)	7.9	12.7	12.7
Immigration enriches culture	3.9	2.8	2.7
% UK should leave EU	12	35	50
Scottish referendum (1-5 unless otherwise stated: 1=disagree; 3=neither; 5 agree)			
Scotland gets its fair share from the union	2.3	1.9	2.6
I would be better off in an independent Scotland	3.4	3.5	2.6
Gap between rich and poor would shrink after independence	3.8	3.6	2.9
'Yes' campaign had a vision for an independent Scotland	4.1	4.2	3.4
Satisfied with British democracy	1.6	1.7	2.2
Satisfied with Scottish democracy	2.8	2.8	2.3
Approve of Scottish government	3.9	3.9	3.1
Feel Scottish	4.2	4.7	4.1
% contacted by the Greens during the referendum campaign	27	11	8
% contacted by the SNP during the referendum campaign	35	41	27
Observations	410	1630	5213

Fig. 3.3 Profile of pro-independence Scottish Green and SNP supporters, October 2014 (Source: British Election Study)

After the referendum, around 31 per cent of the Scottish electorate had both voted for independence and planned on voting for the SNP in the regional list of the 2016 Scottish Parliament election, whereas around eight per cent had both voted for independence and were planning to vote Green at the same election in 2016. As we can see, the Greens have a distinct social profile, tending to be young, male, with or studying for a university degree, non-home owners, non-religious and of a higher social class, although with relatively low household incomes. Particularly interesting is the high level of education and high social class of Scottish Green supporters compared to the SNP's supporters and even the electorate as a whole. Generally, both of these variables tend to be negatively associated with support for Scottish independence (McLean and Thomson 2014). In this sense, the Scottish Greens' support for independence was, in socio-demographic terms, counter-intuitive.

On political values, Greens again form a distinctive group relative to both the SNP's followers and the Scottish electorate. The Greens perceived themselves to be significantly further to the left than SNP supporters–placing themselves at 2.3 on the 0–10 spectrum. However, on specific 'material', left-right issues of redistribution and austerity, the Greens are only slightly more left wing than the SNP's backers, who themselves are further to the left than the Scottish electorate. By contrast, the SNP's supporters have very centrist views on environmentalism, libertarianism, immigration and the EU and, on these issues, the Greens distinguish themselves by their far more radical views. Conversely, the Greens' supporters were more moderate than SNP supporters on questions of Scotland's constitutional status. Greens felt relatively less aggrieved by Scotland's place in the UK and were less sentimentally nationalistic than SNP supporters. The Greens were considerably more likely to believe that independence would reduce inequality rather than make themselves better off, whereas SNP supporters believed both in equal measure. Interestingly, Green supporters after the referendum were far more likely than SNP supporters to have been contacted by Harvie's party during the referendum campaign.

While there are clear patterns in *how* Green supporters varied from SNP supporters following the referendum, we also want to know *why* they chose the Greens. Fig. 3.4 shows logistic regression analyses of the determinants of Green support, rather than SNP support, using the same data as above (for information on operationalisation, see Chap. 6). There is some evidence that youth, education, lack of religion, higher social class and *lower* household incomes predict Green support–though this evidence

	Model 1: Socio Demographic	*Model 2: Political Values*	*Model 3: Scotland Attitudes*	*Model 4: Combined Model*
Age	0.979***			0.986
Gender (male)	1.111			
Ethnicity (white)	0.886			
University Degree	2.241***			1.072
Homeowner	1.227			
Student	1.301			
No religion	1.645**			1.232
Class (ref: missing)				
Higher professional	1.101			1.041
Lower professional	0.883			1.039
Small employer / Intermediate	0.541*			0.679
Routine / Semi-routine	0.451*			0.616
Income (ref: refused to answer)				
£45,000+	0.806			0.993
£30,000-£44,999	1.396			1.409
£15,000-£29,999	1.173			1.046
£0-£14,999	1.741*			1.181
Govt should redistribute		0.880		
Public spending cuts too far		0.843		
Enviro protection too far		0.596***		0.568***
Authoritarian-Libertarian Index		0.864***		0.924**
Immigration enriches culture		1.160*		1.413***
UK should leave EU		0.850		
Scotland fair share from UK			1.676***	1.682***
Ind. would make me better off			0.718**	0.689**
Ind. would reduce inequality			1.076	
'Yes' had a positive vision			0.734***	0.761*
Feel Scottish			0.729***	0.810***
Satisfied with UK democracy			0.819	
Satisfied with Scottish democracy			1.446**	1.334
Approve of Scottish govt			0.735**	0.514***
Green campaign contact			3.531***	2.572***
SNP campaign contact			0.614**	0.656
Constant	0.315*	6.447***	7.224**	35.5***
Pseudo R2	0.090	0.15	0.15	0.31
Observations	1,707	1,734	1,618	1,306

*** $p<0.001$, ** $p<0.01$, * $p<0.05$; Odds Ratios Reported

Fig. 3.4 Determinants of support for Scottish Greens rather than SNP among pro-independence voters (Source: British Election Study, October 2014)

disappears when controlling for political attitudes and attitudes to Scotland. Environmentalism, libertarianism and pro-immigration sentiment all increased the likelihood of Green support, whereas there is no evidence that classic left-wing and anti-austerity attitudes led pro-independence Scots to support the Greens rather than the SNP. Respondents were also drawn to the Greens because they felt less Scottish, disapproved of the incumbent Scottish government, were less impressed by the 'Yes' campaign, did not see the Union as unfair in *national* terms, and did not see independence as a route to personal enrichment. Finally, Greens made their choice of party following the referendum because Harvie's party had actively contacted them during the referendum campaign. It is worth noting that these variables only manage to explain 29 per cent of the variation in choice between the Greens and SNP, suggesting that a considerable portion of the explanation for party choice following the referendum remains unsettled.

The estimated effects of a one standard deviation increase of the statistically significant variables in the combined model are shown in descending order of magnitude in Fig. 3.5.

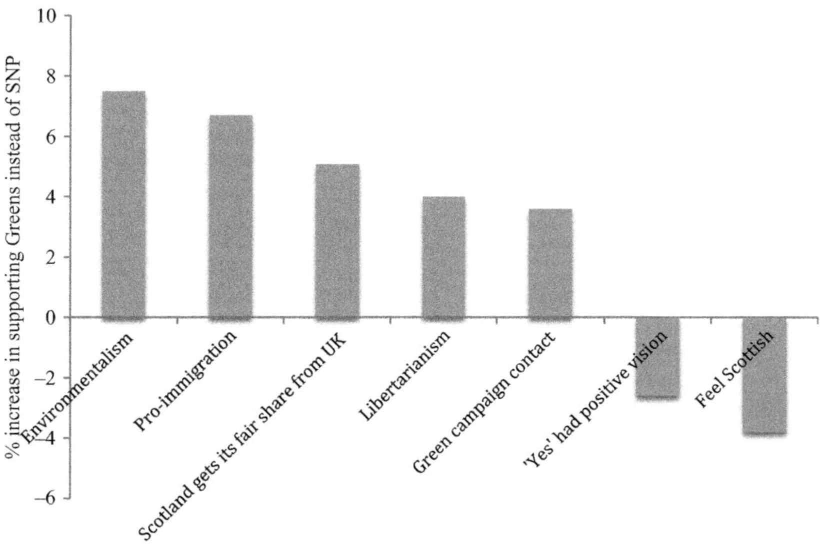

Fig. 3.5 Estimated effects on supporting the Greens rather than the SNP amongst pro-independence voters (Source: British Election Study, October 2014)

Overall, in the run-up to Scotland's September 2014 independence referendum, the Greens consolidated their position as the foremost pro-independence alternative to the SNP and distinguished themselves by outlining a vision for a radical new state. The Greens explicitly rejected independence in the name of nationalism or in order to 'undercut' the rest of the UK on corporation tax, instead justifying independence as a more promising route to social justice than the Westminster government. Armed with a distinctive message, the Greens followed a campaigning strategy that offered them relevance by aligning with the mainstream 'Yes Scotland' campaign while, through other activities, emphasising their own distinctiveness. In doing so, the party placed itself well to capture a portion of the release of political energy that followed the referendum, as pro-independence Scots looked to party membership as a way to express their unwillingness to accept the result as a final defeat for their cause. While most would join the SNP, those with more environmentalist, libertarian, pro-immigration and less nationalistic views would instead be attracted to the Greens, particularly if they had been contacted by the Greens during the referendum campaign or disapproved of the SNP government in Edinburgh. Though Green supporters were more left wing in economic terms than SNP supporters, there is no evidence that this was as important a factor in their choice between the two parties. Greater prominence and funding from the Greens' membership surge would secure the party's position in Scotland's transforming party system, exemplified by their inclusion in the Smith Commission. The party will likely enjoy increased seats in future Scottish Parliament elections though not in the first-past-the-post UK general elections, a situation reinforced by the party's allocation of resources almost entirely to the former election.

Notes

1. BBC News (2014), 'European Elections: Green Party launches campaign', accessed at http://www.bbc.co.uk/news/uk-politics-27187427 on 27/01/2016.
2. Interview with Tom Beckett on 27/11/2015.
3. Blue&green tomorrow (2014), 'British public's concern for the environment 'highest for six years'', accessed at http://blueandgreentomorrow.com/2014/02/25/british-publics-concern-for-the-environment-highest-for-six-years/ on 09/04/2016.

4. YouGovt (2015), Most Important Issues tracker, accessed at https://d25d2506sfb94s.cloudfront.net/cumulus_uploads/document/0g3zhv6y3h/YG-Archives-Pol-Trackers-Issues(2)-Most-important-issues-260515.pdf on 07/04/2014.
5. Marshall, H. (2014), 'Green Party see red with petition against BBC's 'media blackout' and 'UKIP hysteria' – nearing 40,000 supporters', accessed at http://www.mancunianmatters.co.uk/content/300569197-green-party-see-red-petition-against-bbcs-media-blackout-and-ukip-hysteria-%E2%80%93 on 30/01/2016.
6. BBC News (2014), 'European Elections: Green Party launches campaign', accessed at http://www.bbc.co.uk/news/uk-politics-27187427 on 27/01/2016; Bennett, O. (2014), '"UKIP's divisive politics are driving voters to the Greens," says party leader', accessed at http://www.express.co.uk/news/uk/475832/Ukip-s-divisive-politics-are-driving-voters-to-Greens-says-party-leader-Natalie-Bennett on 30/01/2016; Carrington, D. (2014), 'Greens pitch radical renationalization of railways to boost election hopes', accessed at http://www.theguardian.com/environment/2014/may/19/green-party-railways-renationalisation-local-european-elections on 30/01/2016.
7. The Economic Voice (2014), 'Greens now third party amongst students', accessed at http://www.economicvoice.com/greens-now-third-party-amongst-students/ on 30/01/2016.
8. Bennett, O. (2014), 'UKIP's divisive politics are driving voters to the Greens,' says party leader', accessed at http://www.express.co.uk/news/uk/475832/Ukip-s-divisive-politics-are-driving-voters-to-Greens-says-party-leader-Natalie-Bennett on 09/04/2016.
9. Ofcom (2015), 'Review of Ofcom list of major political parties for elections taking place on 7 May 2015', accessed at http://stakeholders.ofcom.org.uk/binaries/consultations/major-parties-15/statement/Major_Parties_Statement.pdf on 21/06/2016.
10. Forsyth, J. (2014), 'How Ed Miliband lost his winning hand', accessed at http://www.spectator.co.uk/2014/11/how-ed-miliband-lost-his-winning-hand/ on 08/04/2016.
11. Jones, J (2007) 'Leading Edge: No', accessed at http://www.theguardian.com/society/2007/sep/12/ guardiansocietysupplement.greenpolitics on 13 June 2015
12. The Green Party (2015), 'The Green Party's Core Values', accessed at https://policy.greenparty.org.uk/core-values.html on 28/01/2016.
13. Green Party (2011), *Target to Win: How to Do It*, accessed at https://my.greenparty.org.uk/resource/how-target-win-ttw on 10/04/2016.
14. Tatchell, P. (2007), 'Green is the new red', accessed at http://www.redpepper.org.uk/green-is-the-new-red/ on 28/01/2016.

15. Scottish Greens vote share in General Elections: 1997: 0.6 per cent; 2001:0.2; 2005:1.1; 2010:0.7; 2015:1.3. Green Party of England and Wales vote share in General Elections: 1997:0.4 per cent; 2001:0.7; 2005:1.1; 2010:1.0; 2015; 4.3.
16. Scottish Green vote share in European Elections: 1994: 1.6 per cent; 1999: 5.8; 2004: 6.8; 2009: 7.3; 2014: 8.1. Green Party of England and Wales vote share in European Elections: 1994: 3.4; 1999: 7.1; 2004: 7.1; 2009: 9.1; 2014: 7.8.
17. Ballard, M. (2012), 'Great Green Campaigns: Scotland 2003' at http://bright-green.org/2012/03/22/greatgreencampaignsscotland2003/, accessed on 10/02/2016.
18. *ibid.*
19. SPICe Briefing (2003), 'Election 2003', accessed at http://www.scottish.parliament.uk/SPICeResources/Research%20briefings%20and%20fact%20sheets/sb03-25.pdf on 10/02/2016.
20. Johnson, S. (2012), 'Greens pull out of Yes Scotland referendum campaign', accessed at http://www.telegraph.co.uk/news/uknews/scotland/9326575/Greens-pull-out-of-Yes-Scotland-referendum-campaign.html on 11/2/2016.
21. Gordon, T. (2012), 'Green ditch SNP 'puppet' fears and join the Yes Scotland campaign', accessed at http://www.heraldscotland.com/news/13076014.Greens_ditch_SNP__puppet__fears_and_join_the_Yes_Scotland_campaign/ on 11/02/2016.
22. Gordon, T. (2014), '"We should leave Britain … it only works for the rich"', accessed at http://www.heraldscotland.com/news/13147220._We_should_leave_Britain_____it_only_works_for_the_rich_/ on 11/2/2016.
23. Gordon, T. (2014), '"We should leave Britain … it only works for the rich"', accessed at http://www.heraldscotland.com/news/13147220._We_should_leave_Britain_____it_only_works_for_the_rich_/ on 11/2/2016.
24. Panelbase (2013), "How much do you agree or disagree with the following statement? … In reaching my decision about whether to support Scottish independence, the prospect of a fairer and more equal society is more important to me than whether Scotland as a while would be slightly richer or slightly poorer.", accessed at http://www.panelbase.com/news/GreenPartyforpublication09042013.pdf on 20/01/2016.
25. Chakelian, A. (2014), 'Leader of the Scottish Greens: "You don't need to like Alex Salmond to vote Yes"', accessed at http://www.newstatesman.com/politics/2014/08/leader-scottish-greens-you-don-t-need-alex-salmond-vote-yes on 20/02/2016.
26. Pauling, T. (2014), 'Green leader claims independence good for the British Isles', accessed at https://www.pressandjournal.co.uk/fp/news/politics/referendum/310724/green-leader-claims-independence-good-for-the-british-isles/ on 30/04/2016.

27. STV (2014), 'Green Party set out 'bold' vision for an independent Scotland', accessed at http://news.stv.tv/tayside/270616-green-party-set-out-bold-vision-for-an-independent-scotland/ on 20/01/2016.
28. Herald Scotland (2014), 'Greens: Yes vote could help Scotland find bold economic alternative', accessed at http://www.heraldscotland.com/news/13154112.Greens__Yes_vote_could_help_Scotland_find_bold_economic_alternatives/ n 20/01/2016.
29. STV (2014), 'Yes and No campaigns clash in key debate on independence referendum', accessed at http://stv.tv/news/politics/news/290654-final-tv-debate-takes-place-in-edinburgh-ahead-of-independence-referendum/ on 03/03/2016.
30. What Scotland Thinks (2016), 'Are you satisfied or dissatisfied with Patrick Harvie as Scottish Green Party leader?', accessed at http://whatscotlandthinks.org/questions/are-you-satisfied-or-dissatisfied-with-patrick-harvie-as-scottish-green-party-1#line on 20/01/2016.
31. Scottish Greens (@scotgp). 'Since yesterday morning, we've gained 1,200 new members. At one point folks were signing up one every 15 seconds! http://www.scottishgreens.org.uk/join-donate/' 20 September 2014. 3:36 am. Tweet.
32. Scottish Greens (@scotgp). 'As of 4pm today, we've added 2,000 new members. Yeah, I said 2,000! Welcome, all!' 20 September 2014. 10:08 am. Tweet.

Bibliography

Bale, T. (2012), 'Supplying the Insatiable Demand: Europe's Populist Radical Right' in *Government and Opposition*, 47 (2), 256–274

Bennie, L. (2004), *Understanding Political Participation: Green Party Membership in Scotland*, Farnham: Ashgate

Bornschier, S. (2010) Cleavage politics and the populist right: the new cultural conflict in Western Europe. Philadelphia: Temple University Press

Bornschier, S. and Kriesi, H. (2012) 'The populist right, the working class, and the changing face of class politics' in Class Politics and the Radical Right (ed. Rydgren, J.). Oxford: Routledge, 10–30

Burchell, J. (2002), *The Evolution of Green Politics: Development & Change within European Green Parties*, London: Earthscan

Burnside, R., Herbert, S., and Curtis, S. (2003) 'Election 2003', SPICe Briefing

Clark, P. B. and Wilson, J. Q. (1961), 'Incentive system: A theory of organization' in *Administrative Science Quarterly*, 6, 129–166.

Fieldhouse, E., J. Green., G. Evans., H. Schmitt, C. van der Eijk, J. Mellon & C. Prosser (2016) British Election Study Internet Panel Waves 1–9.

Ford, R., Goodwin, M. and Cutts, D. (2012), 'Strategic Eurosceptics and polite xenophobes: Support for the United Kingdom Independence Party (UKIP) in the 2009 European Parliament elections' in *European Journal of Political Research*, 51, 204–234

Franklin, M. and Curtice, J. (1996), 'Britain: Opening Pandora's Box' in eds. Van der Eijk, C. and Franklin, M., *Choosing Europe? The European Electorate and National Politics in the Face of Union*. Ann Arbor: University of Michigan Press, 78–96

Goodwin, M. and Milazzo, C. (2015), *UKIP: Inside the Campaign to Redraw the Map of British Politics*, Oxford: Oxford University Press

Heath, A., McLean, I., Taylor, B. and Curtice, J. (1999), 'Between First and Second Order: A Comparison of Voting Behaviour in European and Local Elections in Britain' in *European Journal of Political Research*, 35 (3), 389–414.

Hix, S. and Marsh, M. (2011), 'Second-Order Effects Plus Pan-European Political Swings: An Analysis of European Parliament Elections Across Time' in *Electoral Studies*, 30(1), 4–15.

Inglehart, R. (1971) 'The Silent Revolution in Europe: Intergenerational Change in Post-industrial Societies' in American Political Science Review, 65 (December): 991–1017

Kroh, M., van der Brug, W. and van der Eijk, C. (2007), 'Prospects for Electoral Change' in eds. van der Brug, W. and van der Eijk, C., *European Elections and Domestic Politics. Lessons from the Past and Scenarios for the Future*, Notre Dame: University of Notre Dame Press, 209–225

Lucardie, P. and Rihoux, B. (2008), 'From Amateur-Activists to Professional-Electoral Parties? On the Organizational Transformation of Green Parties in Western Democracies' in eds. Frankland, E. G., Lucardie, P., and Rihoux, B., *Green Parties in Transition*, Farnham: Surrey, 3–18

McLean, C. and Thomson, D. (2014), 'Characterisation of the Disadvantages: Explaining Differences in Levels of Support for Independence by Income Levels, Economic Activity and Socio-Economic Status' in *Scottish Affairs*, 125–147

Mitchell, J. (2015), 'Sea Change in Scotland' in *Parliamentary Affairs*, 68 (suppl 1), 88–100

Reif, K. and Schmitt, H. (1980), 'Nine Second-Order National Elections – A Conceptual Framework for the Analysis of European Election Results' in *European Journal of Political Research*, 8(1), 3–44

Richardson, D. and Rootes, C. (eds) (1995) The Green Challenge: The Development of Green Parties in Europe. London: Routledge

Rihoux, B. and Frankland, E. G. (2008), 'Conclusion: The Metamorphosis of Amateur-Activist Newborns into Professional-Activist Centaurs' in eds. Frankland, E. G., Lucardie, P., and Rihoux, B., *Green Parties in Transition*. Farnham: Surrey, 259–288

Rüdig, W. (2008), 'Green Party Organization in Britain: Continuity and Change' in eds. Frankland, E. G., Lucardie, P., and Rihoux, B., *Green Parties in Transition*. Farnham: Surrey, 199–224

van der Eijk, C., Franklin, M. and Marsh, M. (1996), 'What Voters Teach Us About Europe-Wide Elections: What Europe-Wide Elections Teach Us About Voters' in *Electoral Studies*, 15 (2), 149–166

Whiteley, P.F. and Sanders, D., British Election Study, 2010: Face-to-Face Survey [computer file]. Colchester, Essex: UK Data Archive [distributor], August 2014.

CHAPTER 4

'Green Surge': Becoming England's Third Largest Party

Abstract The Green Party underwent a rapid increase in membership in late 2014 and early 2015, quadrupling in size and becoming the third largest party in England. The catalyst for this 'Green Surge' was the party's exclusion from the pre-election televised leaders debates–in contrast to the inclusion of UKIP for the first time–which was seen by much of the electorate as unjust. Those who joined the party had remarkably similar political attitudes to the Greens' pre-existing members, suggesting that the 'Surgers' were motivated to join by ideological affinity. In particular, both shared antipathy towards austerity, the current state of British politics and the major parties, as well as highly pro-immigration and libertarian outlooks. Joining the party became a medium of dissent for a certain political group, not only against the decision regarding the debates but also against a perceived rightward drift in British politics. The Greens were able to capitalise on this phenomenon because of earlier internal changes in their membership and communications operations. As a result the party gained far greater financial resources from membership fees and a number of high-profile donations, allowing it to stand in double the number of Westminster constituencies that it had five years earlier.

Keywords Election debates • Green Surge • Party membership • Party finances • Political donations

J. Dennison, *The Greens in British Politics*,
DOI 10.1007/978-3-319-42673-0_4

The Debate Over the Debates

In May 2014, David Cameron announced that the inclusion of the GPEW in the 2015 pre-election televised leaders debates was a pre-requisite for his own participation.[1] The Greens' presence had, until that point, not even been in consideration in the drawn-out discussions over which parties would participate. The central point of contention, instead, had been whether or not UKIP's high-flying leader, Nigel Farage, should be included–a prospect that the Prime Minister opposed but seemed increasingly likely. Cameron, who had fared poorly in the 2010 election debates, was particularly eager to avoid directly confronting the unpredictable UKIP leader on the issue of immigration, which, in spite of Conservative manifesto pledges, had reached record highs. Cameron calculated that demanding the Greens' inclusion would hurt Labour if the debates took place, or, even better, lead to negotiations collapsing and no debates taking place whatsoever– his preferred outcome.

The controversy over the debates continued throughout the summer of 2014 and gave the GPEW unprecedented exposure. This coverage caught the party at a particularly strong moment, having just increased its number of seats in the European and local elections and finished ahead of the Liberal Democrats, as well as having a message that was, by Green standards, unusually salient in the wider electorate. During this period, journalists, few of whom had discussed the party before, enthusiastically began to portray the Greens as a potential 'UKIP of the Left'. Indeed, media coverage of the GPEW followed the same pattern as that of candidates in American presidential primary elections–'discovery, scrutiny and decline'. This sequence (Sides and Vavreck 2013: 41–42) has its roots in a combination of, on the one hand, a field of candidates that fails to inspire enthusiasm, leaving many voters undecided and eager to hear of alternatives, and, on the other hand, a lengthy 'long campaign' giving reporters the challenge to "produce newsworthy events or moments every day." After the introduction of the Fixed Term Parliaments Act (2011), the 2015 UK electoral campaign had the potential for extensive 'horse race' media coverage more akin to American elections. This, along with the ambivalence of the electorate towards the major parties, made the Greens–novel and anti-establishment–an obvious subject for a media keen for UKIP-style stories of an insurgent party during a summer of relatively few newsworthy events.

The idea of a left-wing insurgent party, given additional prominence by Cameron's use of the party in negotiations about the pre-election leaders debates, was enough for media outlets to increase their coverage of Bennett's party. News stories during this period tended to avoid details of policies or potential shortcomings in the party and instead speculated about the Greens' rise, their strengths and the potential impact they could have on the election. Typical headlines included "Potential support for the Greens outweighs potential support for UKIP",[2] "Rise of Green party and UKIP … have killed the old order and all bets are off", the Greens as the "third insurgent force",[3] "A new "people's army"? "How the Greens could be set to become the new UKIP",[4] "Here come the Greens"[5] and the UK now having a "five-party system" (Dennison 2015).[6] Like in American primaries, the increase in news coverage preceded a boost in poll ratings (Slides and Vavreck 2013: 43), which remained static for the Greens over the summer.

In October, the television broadcasters proposed the exact scenario that Cameron wished to avoid–a four-party debate including UKIP but excluding the Greens. It was only then that the GPEW's poll ratings and membership figures began to dramatically increase. Immediately the party protested the decision as unjust and undemocratic. Caroline Lucas, Green MP, tweeted, "Taking legal advice over Green exclusion from TV debates. Apparently 'messy' to have too many candidates. Democracy IS messy – sort it out!"[7] An online petition calling for the Greens' inclusion collected 30,000 signatures overnight, suggesting that there was a latent pool of sympathy towards the party. The petition, set up by an undergraduate student and eventually signed by 280,000 people, echoed Lucas' arguments and framed the issue in terms of gender equality–"Natalie Bennett has just as much a right to be on that panel as the men … By excluding a party with a female leader, we are sending a clear message to the public–politics is still an old boys club."[8] The Greens would also frame their exclusion as a gender issue, later producing a poster of Caroline Lucas and Natalie Bennett with beaming smiles above the "teasing" slogan 'What are you afraid of, boys?'[9]

The public and media treated the Greens' exclusion as a legitimate grievance. One poll showed that 80 per cent of the electorate were in favour of including the Greens.[10] "The perception was that we were being victimised and marginalised through the lack of invitation to the leader debates", remembers Shahrar Ali, GPEW Deputy Leader. Aside from issues of fairness, the inclusion of UKIP, who by this point were by far the most divisive party in British politics,[11] ensured that the controversy aroused particular passion. "UKIP was going to be on there and we weren't", remembers Jean Lambert MEP, which "also meant that if you were somebody … who really wanted to put two fingers up to UKIP, signing the petition was the way to do it."

The enthusiasm of the media towards the Greens, typical of the 'discovery' phase of media coverage, was accelerated as "polls and news coverage reinforced each other, as good poll numbers became a rationale for additional coverage" (Sides and Vavreck 2013: 43). Quickly the phrase 'Green Surge' was taken up to describe the sudden increase in Green poll ratings and membership. Stories simply summarising the Greens' improved polling and membership figures such as "Greens ahead of Liberal Democrats in YouGov poll" were typical of the period and tended to link the polling increase to "intensified pressure for the Greens to be represented in a general election TV debates."[12] Tantalisingly, the BBC responded to a Green Party letter demanding their inclusion by stating that they would "continue to keep any new evidence of increased support for the Green Party under close review."[13] By mid-November the Labour Party were sufficiently concerned by the growth of the Greens to set up an 'anti-Green unit' led by shadow minister Sadiq Khan, who focused on portraying the Green control of Brighton City Council as disastrous and, most importantly, Ed Miliband as genuinely left wing and a clean break from the New Labour years.[14] Such manoeuvres did not appear to have any impact on the Greens' poll ratings, which continued rising from their summer average of around four per cent to over seven per cent by Christmas. Furthermore, between the broadcasters' announcement and the end of the year, the GPEW membership shot up from 20,000 to over 30,000.

In the New Year, Ofcom, Britain's communications and television regulator, opened a draft consultation arguing against the Greens' entitlement to party election broadcasts on the major television and radio networks because they were not considered to be a major party. UKIP, on the other hand, were now considered a major party. Though separate from the television debates issue, the draft consultation undermined the Greens' legal challenge to be included in the far more important television debates. However, rather than resigning themselves to defeat, the Greens, delighted by their unprecedented publicity, refused to back down and framed Ofcom's consultation as further evidence of discrimination against the only female-led and anti-austerity party, as well as being an apologetic stance by the establishment towards Nigel Farage's populist right party. Furthermore, Ofcom's final decision on which parties would have 'major party' status, following the consultation, was scheduled to be made in March, thus protracting the controversy even further.

Throughout January, an unlikely alliance of the GPEW, sympathetic members of the public and the Conservative Party, combined with a keen media, ensured that the topic remained in the news. "We had people from all sorts of places, regardless of their political persuasion–[English film director] Danny Boyle famously–supporting the call for us to be included in the debates, because it just wasn't seen as fair", remembers GPEW National Campaigns Director Chris Luffingham. One Conservative MPs slammed the "disgraceful, indefensible decision by Ofcom" while Cameron reaffirmed his stance that he would not take part unless the Greens were involved and that he was "quite happy for there to be no debates at all."[15, 16] Moreover, so long as the debates controversy remained in the news, the Green Party continued to receive extensive coverage. Reflecting on the increased media coverage of the Green Party, Luffingham goes on to acknowledge that "a lot of it was down to the debates because it was a major, major news story for everybody, not just us, ... because Cameron was deciding whether he was going to do it or not. There was a lot of news around it. And that played a large part in our increased media exposure."

More importantly for the GPEW, following the Ofcom consultation, their polling figures and membership numbers skyrocketed. In just a single week the Greens added 13,000 new members to their ranks, taking their total to 46,000 by 21 January and making them England's third largest party. One new member, having paid the £31 to join, explained her decision in terms of opposition to UKIP and left-wing economics: "I hate the idea of Nigel Farage standing up there, and not Natalie Bennett ... I like the fact that they stand up for things that are important. Like, I don't think we should have privatised railways."[17] Charlotte George, 2015 Green parliamentary candidate for Hackney South and Shoreditch, recounts how new members in her constituency explicitly pointed to the debate controversy as the catalyst for them joining, with one stating "I'm just so pissed off about the debates, that you guys weren't invited."

The internal party reaction to the Green Surge was a mix of satisfaction and shock. Some party members felt that the massive increase in membership was due primarily to vast forces out of their control. Brian Heatley, co-author of the 2010 and 2015 manifestos, compares the party during this period to "a cork bobbing in the sea. ... You'd find the cork rise out of the water a little more, or a little less, by things we did. But the overall height we got to was to do with much grander things that were going on, and not much to do with us." Adam Ramsay, who had contributed to the Greens on both sides of the border, similarly remembers the Green Surge as surprising, "like you booked a massive hall for your birthday party and until two o'clock only a couple of your friends had come and you were sitting around at the bar feeling a bit miserable and all of a sudden 2,000 people arrive. It was very emotional." However, Ramsay also believes that the Surge was at least partially the result of the party's move to the left and on-going 'professionalisation'. Indeed, recent internal changes made them far more prepared to capitalise on their increased profile when such an event as the controversy over the debates erupted. Mark Cridge, GPEx Management Coordinator, is unequivocal in his belief that the party made the Green Surge happen, confidently stating, "we've had political surges before but they've always fallen back because the infrastructure wasn't in place, so that was intentional, that wasn't getting lucky."

On 23 January, long before Ofcom's scheduled decision on the election broadcasts, the television networks relented to David Cameron's wishes and announced plans for two seven-party television debates, including the original four parties as well as the GPEW, the SNP and Plaid Cymru. Around the same time, the Green Party's poll ratings began to fall fairly rapidly. As we shall see in the next chapter, this was not only a result of their inclusion in the debates but was primarily caused by the more intensive scrutiny that the media gave the Greens once their participation was ensured. The GPEW's membership continued to grow after their inclusion in the debates, albeit at a slower rate of 6,000 new members in February, 3,000 in March and another 7,000 in April and early May. The continuing rise in membership underlines the fact that the debates were not the sole cause of the Green Surge but instead were a necessary trigger to draw attention to the party and the gulf in ideology, policies and personnel–most notably in terms of gender–between the GPEW and their rivals. Once this trigger occurred, the social and purposive incentives to join the party–specifically in terms of ensuring the Greens were included in the debates and more broadly as an expression over the state of British politics–continued to increase and were clarified by greater coverage of the party.

Who Were the Surgers and Why Did They Join?

By investigating the socio-demographic and attitudinal profile of those who joined the GPEW in 2014 and early 2015 we can better understand what caused the Green Surge. Furthermore, we can also compare these individuals to those who had joined the party earlier, to appreciate how the Green Surge changed the party. In order to do this, I use data from the Party Members Project (PMP) (Bale et al. 2015).[18] Their project compares the membership profiles of six British political parties–the Conservatives, the GPEW, Labour, the Liberal Democrats, the SNP and UKIP.

The first round of surveys, all of which were carried out online, took place during the summer after the 2015 General Election and asked questions about the respondent's background, attitudes to politics and attitudes to their party. In total, 845 Green Party members responded to the survey. For the purposes of this analysis, I split the respondents into three cohorts based on their date of joining: Pre-2010 (12 per cent of Greens), 2010–2013 (15 per cent) and 2014–2015 (73 per cent), with the latter constituting the 'Surgers'.[19]

Where possible, I also compare the findings from this project to those of a separate independent survey of Green Party members also carried out that summer (Rüdig 2015). This second survey forms part of the comparative European Green Party Membership Survey (EGPM), which seeks to survey members of all of Europe's Green parties on similar topics to that of the PMP, namely socio-demographics, political attitudes and assessments of the party. Over 8,000 members responded to the survey, considerably more than the number of GPEW members who responded to the PMP. Rüdig also offers comparisons between the findings of the EGPM survey and other studies of the GPEW carried out in 1984, 1990, 2002 and 2009. The findings of this survey were released in July of 2015 and, within the current membership, compared Surgers with pre-Surgers. While this is an extremely useful analysis, some of the results of which are replicated in the PMP survey, I will show that it is important to highlight the variation between those who joined prior to 2010 and those who joined afterwards, between 2010 and 2013, and the Surgers who joined between 2014 and 2015. It should be stressed that Rüdig's findings are preliminary and thus should be interpreted with caution (Fig. 4.1).

How did the Green Surge change the socio-demographic profile of the Green Party? The Green Surge had the effect of lowering the average age of the party to the point where it was significantly younger than the electorate as a whole. However, in reality this process had already been started by the 2010–2013 cohort, whose average age, at 43, was little higher than the Surgers' average age. Furthermore, while the pre-2010 cohort's average age in 2015 was 51, their average age upon joining was just 35, suggesting that a significant portion of this cohort had been in the party for many years. This supports Rüdig's observation that "the party experienced a clear aging process between the 1980s and the 2000s. The Green Surge appears to have helped in arresting this process" (Rüdig 2015: 4).

	Pre-2010	2010-2013	2014-2015	N	Electorate
Socio Demographics					
Mean age	51	43	41	845	46
Mean age when joined the party	35	40	40	841	-
% male	56	66	56	845	50
% white British	87	91	89	845	90
% graduates	66	61	55	832	26
% lower social classes (C2DE)[i]	29	35	36	845	46
% higher social classes (ABC1)	71	65	64	845	54
% home owners	71	51	63	287	73
% atheist/agnostic	55	59	58	229	45
Left-right placement (0-10 left to right)					
Self-placement	2.2	1.7	1.9	833	5.1
Placement of parties:					
Greens	2.3	1.9	2.0	839	2.8
Conservatives	8.4	8.6	8.4	841	7.8
Labour	5.3	5.2	5.1	840	3.1
Liberal Democrats	5.7	5.8	5.5	826	4.8
UKIP	9.2	9.2	9.2	835	7.7
Policy Attitudes (1-5 disagree to agree)[ii]					
Government should redistribute incomes	4.5	4.6	4.5	840	3.5
Cuts to public spending have gone too far	4.6	4.7	4.7	837	3.7
Schools should teach children to obey authority	2.6	2.2	2.6	841	4.0
Censorship of media is necessary to uphold moral standards	2.3	2.0	2.2	839	3.3
Immigration good for the economy	4.1	4.4	4.2	836	2.7
Immigration enriches British culture	4.1	4.4	4.3	832	2.6
% would vote to stay in the EU	84	86	84	822	58
Attitudes to politics (1-5 disagree to agree)					
Politicians don't care what people like me think	3.7	3.9	3.8	839	3.5
When the party members work together, they can really change the local community or the country	3.3	3.1	3.2	816	-
Membership of other groups					
% member of Greenpeace[iii]	20	25	14	845	0.3
% member of the World Wildlife Fund[iv]	6	2	4	845	1.5
Attitudes to the GPEW					
% leadership should have more policy influence	3	2	5	845	-
% membership should have more policy influence	17	24	27	845	-
% member of an internal party group	20	22	9	845	-

Fig. 4.1 Profiles of Green Party of England and Wales members by cohort and electorate profile (Source: Party Members Project; British Election Study 2014–2017)

The Surgers were 56 per cent male and so diminished, though did not eradicate, the party membership's gender imbalance. In fact, the Surgers had the same gender ratio as those who joined the party prior to 2010 but were far more likely to be female than members of the 2010–2013 cohort, who were 66 per cent male. Again, these findings are supported by Rüdig's survey, which also shows that the Green Surge improved but did not rectify the over-representation of men within the party.

In terms of ethnicity, 89 per cent of 'Surgers' were 'White British', a slightly higher proportion than the pre-2010 cohort though lower than the more ethnically homogenous 2010–2013 cohort. These numbers are in line with the ethnic profile of the electorate, unlike those of Rüdig's survey, which show that 95 per cent of both pre-Surge and Surge members were 'white', possibly resulting from a high proportion of 'white non-British' members.

Both the educational and class profile of the three cohorts of GPEW members show that the party has diversified its socio-demographic membership since 2010. The percentage of pre-2010, 2010–2013 and Green Surge members who have degrees is 66, 61 and 55 respectively, although when current students are excluded, the latter figure rises to 61. The party remains far more educated than the electorate as a whole, only 26 per cent of whom are graduates. In terms of professional class, the Green Surge and the 2010–2013 cohort both contributed to creating a party more reflective of the electorate as a whole. While 71 per cent of the pre-2010 cohort belonged to higher social groups (professionals, managers, supervisors, clerks and administrative workers) only 64 per cent of the Surgers belonged to these groups. Conversely, the proportion of members belonging to lower social groups (skilled, semi-skilled and unskilled manual work, state pensioners, casual workers and those unemployed with only state benefits) rises by cohort from 29 to 35 to 36 per cent respectively, though still well below the national average of 46 per cent. Although the party has become more societally representative in professional and managerial terms, it has moved away from the electorate in terms of home owning. The pre-2010 cohort (71 per cent) were already slightly less likely than the electorate (73 per cent) to own a home and the 2010–2013 cohort and Surgers are even less likely at 51 and 63 per cent respectively. More than ever, the GPEW is a party of home renters rather than homeowners.

Rüdig's report finds similar changes in the educational profile of the Greens but does not report on the social class of Green members nor on their home ownership. The findings of the PMP contradict his conclusion that "the 'Green Surge' has not fundamentally changed the make-up of the Green Party membership in socio-economic terms" (Rüdig 2015, 6).

The PMP data shows that the GPEW have become significantly more socio-demographically diverse since 2010 in terms of class, education and home ownership, trends that the Surge reinforced.

Onto policy attitudes, the Surgers did not change the average left-right position of the party. When party members were asked to place themselves on a left-right scale of 0–10, the pre-2010 cohort placed themselves at 2.2, the 2010–2013 cohort placed themselves at 1.7, and the Surgers gave an average score of 1.9, which was far to the left of the electorate's average self-placement of 5.1. This supports Rüdig's conclusion (2015: 6) that *overall* "the leftward shift had already occurred before the 'Green Surge'." More specifically, however, the Surgers actually split the difference between the more moderate pre-2010 cohort and the more radical 2010–2013 cohort, creating the illusion of little recent change. In fact, the 0.5 unit difference between the two earlier cohorts is almost as great as the leftward swing in the party between 2002 and 2015–when, according to Rüdig's findings, the party's mean score was 2.7 and 2.1 respectively (2015: 6).

Of equal interest is how the Greens' members perceive the major political parties. In this respect, variation between the cohorts is somewhat limited, though it is noteworthy that each cohort places their party almost exactly where they place themselves. The key variation is between the Green membership and the electorate. Most fascinatingly, the Greens view their party as the *only* significant left of centre party in England. GPEW members on average see Labour as a centre-right party, giving them a score of between 5.3 and 5.1 on the left-right spectrum, whereas the electorate as a whole views Labour as a centre-left party and places them at 3.1 on the spectrum. The wide variance here goes someway to not just describing the Green Surge but also explaining it.

The Green Party were able to attract new members who, like their existing members, felt that there was a broad ideological gulf between themselves and all of the mainstream parties, including the Labour Party. The electorate may agree with Green members that the Liberal Democrats could be described as a centrist party or even centre-right party (with voters assigning Nick Clegg's party a 4.8 and GPEW members locating them between 5.5 and 5.8 on the scale) and also could agree that the Conservatives were a right-wing party (respectively placing David Cameron's party at 7.8 and between 8.4 and 8.6). However, those who believed that Miliband's party was a centre-right force seemed to be a highly distinct group and, if they had not joined already, found a natural home in the GPEW during the Green Surge. The other key finding is that Green members of every cohort not only saw UKIP as a right-wing party, as the electorate did, but believed they were a far right force at 9.2 on the 0–10 scale, considerably further to the right than the electorate's assessment of a 7.7 for Nigel Farage's party.

When respondents were asked how much they agreed with specific policy statements, we again see areas of similarity and contrast between the GPEW's membership and the broader electorate, as well as consistent trends in the, generally minor, variation between the three cohorts of members. First, Green members of every cohort are highly pro-immigration, on average either agreeing or agreeing strongly that immigration is good for the economy and that it enriches British culture. The Greens' attitudes towards immigration, however, put them at odds with the generally anti-immigration electorate and more so than on any other major issue. On the related issue of European Union membership, we see a similar pattern. Greens are very pro-EU, with between 84 and 86 per cent saying that they would vote to remain in the case of a referendum on Britain's membership, a much higher proportion than in the general public, of whom only 58 per cent said in May 2015 that they would vote to remain.

Green members are even more united on the issue of austerity than they are on immigration. Each of the three cohorts strongly believes that public spending cuts have 'gone much too far' and tend to express this in the strongest possible terms, on average responding with a 4.7 on the 1–5 scale. The electorate tend to agree that austerity has gone too far but are more moderate, placing themselves between 'about right' and 'gone too far' at 3.7. The GPEW's attitudes to government redistribution of incomes are similar to their views on austerity–each cohort is unequivocally in favour of redistribution whereas the electorate, although still in favour, is more ambiguous.

Regarding issues on the libertarian-authoritarian axis, Green members of every cohort oppose teaching children to obey authority in schools and the censorship of films and magazines. Though their overall opposition is lukewarm, it stands in firm contrast to the views of the electorate, who are particularly in favour of teaching children authority in schools and slightly lean towards favouring censorship of media. As with economic issues, the 2010–2013 cohort is the most radical of the three GPEW member cohorts.

In terms of attitudes to politicians, the GPEW's members are highly dissatisfied. Each cohort is likely to agree with the statement that 'politicians don't care about what people like me think' and more so than the average member of the electorate. When we consider that members of the Greens are politically motivated and interested in politics enough to have joined a party–two traits that tend to be associated with feelings of efficacy–the level of disillusionment with politicians within the Greens' membership is more striking. Even on the issues of internal party efficacy–the belief that 'when the party members work together, they can really change the local community or the country'–members of each cohort place themselves more or less at the centre of the 1–5 scale. On both of these measures, the 2010–2013 cohort is the most disillusioned, the pre-2010 the least, and the Surgers split the difference.

The three cohorts of Green members vary starkly in their membership of other environmental organisations. While 25 per cent of the 2010–2013 cohort are members of radical, environmentalist organisation Greenpeace, only two per cent of this cohort are members of the more traditionalist, conservationist World Wildlife Fund (WWF), little more than the proportion of the general public. By contrast, 20 per cent of the pre-2010 cohort were members of Greenpeace and a full six per cent were members of the WWF. Also of interest is that the Surgers, despite tending to split the difference between the previous two cohorts on ideology, policy attitudes and even socio-demographics, were far less likely to be members of Greenpeace than either previous cohort, at 14 per cent. This suggests that their interest in environmentalism is weaker than that of previous cohorts. Moreover, Rüdig's survey specifically asks whether members joined for environmentalist or social justice reasons. Convincingly, "among members who had joined before 2014, 41 per cent declared to have joined out of concern for the environment and 21 per cent out of concern for social justice". On the other hand, for Surgers, "the figures are 24 per cent joining out of concern for the environment [and] 37 per cent for social justice" (Rüdig 2015: 9). The PMP data on membership of environmentalist organisations, combined with Rüdig's findings, suggest that while many Surgers are environmentalists, social justice is the prime motivation of this cohort.

Finally, we move on to the political histories of each cohort (see Fig. 4.2). Current Green members had little history of voting for their party prior to 2015. In 2005, only 14 per cent of current members voted for the GPEW, with the figure rising to a still small 21 per cent in 2010. By 2015, this figure had risen to 83 per cent – still by no means unanimous.

	Pre-2010	2010-2013	2014-2015	Overall
2005 election[i]				
Did not vote	4	11	11	11
Labour	18	25	37	33
Liberal Democrats	28	43	34	35
Greens	44	13	10	14
Other	6	7	8	7
2010 election				
Did not vote	3	4	9	8
Labour	14	17	20	19
Liberal Democrats	25	39	49	45
Greens	57	31	13	21
Other	2	8	8	8
2015 election				
Did not vote	1	1	2	2
Labour	5	12	14	13
Liberal Democrats	1	1	2	2
Green	93	85	80	83
Other	1	2	4	3

Fig. 4.2 Past voting record of Green Party of England and Wales members by cohort(Source: Party Members Project; note: figures represent only those eligible to vote at the time)

Despite having similar profiles to existing Green Party members, neither the 2010–2013 cohort nor the Surgers voted Green prior to joining them. In fact, GPEW members have a history of either not voting or voting for other parties, even when they have already joined. In 2010, only 57 per cent of *existing* members voted Green. There are a number of possible explanations for this. The GPEW only had sufficient resources to pay for the deposits for party candidates in 182 constituencies in 2005 and 310 in 2010. By 2015, this figure had risen to 573. Members were also likely to have voted tactically in view of Westminster's first-past-the-post electoral system. Furthermore, arguably the Greens were less electorally focused in the past, particularly for House of Commons elections, and were as, if not more, interested in campaigning and activism. Even in 2015, 17 per cent of party members, many of whom had only recently joined, did not vote for the Greens, with most of those instead voting for the Labour Party.

Of the three cohorts' voting records, the voting history of the Surgers is unique (see Fig. 4.2). Whereas both the pre-2010 and 2010–2013 cohorts were far more likely to vote for the Liberal Democrats in prior elections, the Surgers were most likely to vote for Labour in 2005, then Liberal Democrat in 2010, before voting Green in 2015. In this sense, the Surgers offer a mirror image to UKIP voters who also moved from Labour after 2005 to the Conservatives in 2010, before settling on a third party–UKIP–that more authentically articulated their concerns in 2015 (Evans and Mellon 2015). To some extent, the rise of both the Greens and UKIP was caused by the disintegration of the Blairite coalition of anti-immigration, traditionalist working-class voters and libertarian middle-class voters–neither of whom were ultimately satisfied with their 2010 staging posts of the Conservatives and Liberal Democrats, respectively.

To conclude, the Green Surge diversified the GPEW's socio-demographic profile, in terms of age, gender, education, home ownership and class, and reinforced the party membership's ideological position, which had moved sharply leftward between 2010 and 2013. The Surgers, with remarkable similarity to their fellow GPEW members, were stridently pro-immigration, anti-austerity and significantly more libertarian than the electorate. This combination of views on the three ideological axes made the Greens a distinct ideological force in England prior to the 2015 election. The similarity between the GPEW's new and old membership cohorts suggests that the Surgers joined the party because of ideological affinity, as well as out of sympathy regarding the television debates controversy. Of particular interest is that the Surgers, like the other GPEW membership cohorts, viewed their party as *the only* left of centre political party in England. Specifically, the appraisal by Green members that the Labour Party was a centre-right organisation makes the Greens highly distinct from the electorate as a whole. The most common voting history of Surgers was Labour in 2005 and then Liberal Democrat in 2010, suggesting that these individuals had become disenchanted with both of these parties before turning to Natalie Bennett's party. Indeed, given their level of political interest, the Surgers were highly disillusioned with British politics, as were those already in the GPEW. Rather than joining the Greens to alter them, it appears that the Surgers found a natural home in Natalie Bennett's party of pro-immigration, anti-authority, anti-austerity radicals, after what must have seemed like a lifetime in the political wilderness.

Increased Resources From the Surge

The Green Surge directly affected the party's 2015 election performance by bringing in far greater membership fees. Whereas the GPEW's receipts from membership fees in the years 2009 and 2010 were £132,822 and £170,366 respectively, in 2014 membership fees accounted for £431,411 of the party's total income, a figure that further ballooned to an estimated £935,000 in 2015.[20]

Indirectly, the Surge also brought in funds thanks to the increase in donations that the party began to receive. The GPEW was now able to go to potential donors with ambitious projections on the return that their donations could bring in terms of seats. Tom Beckett, Director for Fundraising and Operations, remembers, "basically our big donors said 'we're not going to give you any more money unless you up your ambition.'" In November, in response to donors' demands, GPEx agreed to target 12 first or second places in the General Election and a 20 per cent increase in councillors. This ambitious target necessitated, in turn, higher spending. Tom Beckett goes on to say, "what came with ambition was additional spend. I said 'we've got to be able to sketch out an additional spend if we're going to be able to respond to this ambition. Let's just put in all the things we really, really need and it doesn't even matter if it doesn't balance, let's just do it.' At that stage, in early November, we'd looked at putting together a budget that would drive us into debt by £250,000 by May 2015." From there, the party began to approach large donors with an aim of plugging that financial gap, including donor events with Caroline Lucas.

In total, donations to the GPEW in 2014 and 2015 were a combined £2,000,000, compared to just £770,000 in 2009 and 2010. Of particular note, fashion designer Vivienne Westwood donated over £300,000 to the party in late 2014. Westwood publically supported the Greens' ideological stance and reserved special scorn for the modern Labour Party, stating, "none of the other parties are pro-community. The Labour party used to say it was the people's party; it's exactly the same as the Conservative party. There's not a hair to put between them. The difference is the Green Party is a people's party, they are putting people first and all the other parties put business first."[21] Ironically, just a few months later the Greens would exclude Westwood from any further campaigning activities with the party because of her off-shore tax arrangements.[22]

Drastically increased membership fees, coupled with greater donations as well as other sources of income, meant that the GPEW's total income in 2014 and 2015 was over £4.5 million, three times the corresponding figure for the previous election. The party immediately used the additional funds to hire 12 new full-time employees and made their recently hired Regional Campaigns Coordinators full-time. Whereas the party had only eight full-time members of staff around the time of the 2014 European Parliament elections, that figure reached 50 by the time of the general election. Darren Hall, candidate for Bristol West, argues that 'the big difference was, in the run up to this election, the Green Party had enough capacity and resource at the centre to do a much better job of getting those messages out to the public and having two or three people in London to run a press team made a fundamental difference.' The increased resources from the Surge and the subsequent donations allowed the Greens to have a centralised press strategy, and the wherewithal to implement it, for the first time.

Indeed, the party's 2015 campaign expenditure, at £1,141,905, was three and a half times greater than what it had been in 2010 and seven times what it was in 2005. Caroline Lucas, MP for Brighton Pavilion, recalls, "the finances that were coming in meant that we could be more professional when it came to organising telephone canvassing, getting some of our literature out and we had a really good broadcast." The additional resources also fed into the party's targeted campaigning strategy. "The money essentially allowed us to fund campaign schemes in eight different key constituencies ... to be able to fund billboards ... a social media person and to be able to put together a digital pop up agency and call local parties and start digital campaigns", remembers Tom Beckett. However, Peter Barnett, three-time GPEx member, puts the GPEW's greater financial capabilities into context when remembering, "we had a lot of money to play with. Well, compared to normal, not compared to the large parties." Indeed, the Greens' 2015 spending, though by far their most ever, was still only 40 per cent of the size of UKIP's, nine per cent of Labour's and seven per cent of the Conservative's expenditure (Fig. 4.3).[23]

Finally, thanks to increased funds, the GPEW were able to afford the £500 electoral deposits to stand candidates in 538 of England and Wales' 574 constituencies, nearly double the figure in 2010 and around three times the figure in 2005. Caroline Lucas recalls, "so I think one difference was just the coverage we managed to achieve in terms of candidate standing, which meant that we were much more on the horizons of local press and local people, because nearly everywhere had a Green Party

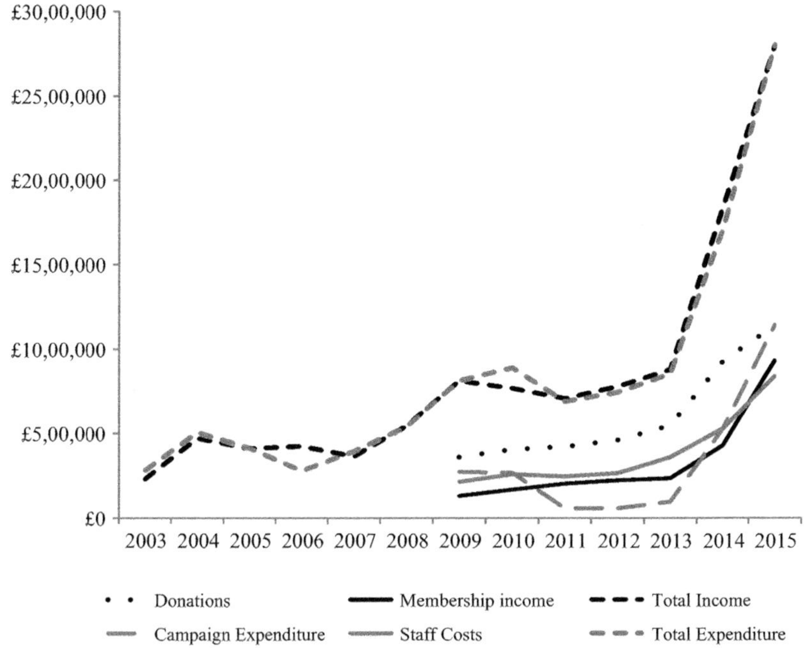

Fig. 4.3 GPEW income and expenditure by year (Source: Electoral Commission)

candidate, which was quite unusual." Notably, the party used online fundraising website Crowdfunder to increase its number of candidates. "It was another massive leap of faith", argues Tom Beckett, "their director is a Green Party member and they wanted to help us. They essentially agreed that they'd set up our page and coach local parties on setting up Crowdfunder platforms. By January or February I think we'd set up 30. By the end of the election we'd done 160, 170. And we were getting all that data into our database. Basically, we used Crowdfunder to stand in as many seats as possible. We'd got onto around 83 per cent before we started this initiative, but then we managed to raise £80,000, raising the numbers to around 91 per cent."

Overall, the Green Surge put the GPEW in a financial position that would allow it to have a truly national general election campaign for the first time, even if it remained overshadowed in scale by the major parties. The Surge swelled the party's coffers via membership fees and increased the prominence and electoral potential of the party enough to interest donors. The net result of these additional forms of income meant that the party was better equipped and staffed at national level and was able to secure full-time presence at regional and, in the case of target constituencies, local level. It also gave more Britons than ever the chance to vote for a Green candidate, as the party no longer had to fear the previously costly impact of losing hundreds of election deposits. In 2015, the GPEW, via sudden membership growth and the ability and ambition to appeal to donors, were able to finally make small steps towards overcoming the British electoral system's vast institutional barriers to entry.

Notes

1. Morris, N. (2014), 'Election 2015: David Cameron suggests five-way debate between party leaders', accessed at http://www.independent.co.uk/news/uk/politics/election-2015-david-cameron-suggests-five-way-debate-between-party-leaders-9347387.html on 30/04/2016.
2. Eaton, G. (2014) 'Potential support for the Greens outweighs potential support for UKIP', accessed at http://www.newstatesman.com/politics/2014/11/potential-support-greens-outweighs-potential-support-ukip on 01/03/2016.
3. Helm, T. (2014) '2015 general election could be the most unpredictable vote in living memory', accessed at http://www.theguardian.com/politics/2014/dec/27/2015-general-election-unpredictable-green-party-ukip on 01/03/2016.
4. Bentley, G. (2014) 'A new "people's army"? How the Greens could be set to become the new UKIP', accessed at http://www.cityam.com/1416586707/new-peoples-army-how-greens-could-be-set-become-new-ukip on 01/03/2016.
5. Payne, S. (2014), 'Green Party up to 11 per cent in latest Ashcroft poll', access at http://blogs.spectator.co.uk/coffeehouse/2015/01/green-party-on-11-per-cent-in-latest-ashcroft-poll/ on 01/03/2016.
6. Goldhill, O. (2014), 'Open Thread: Can British politics survive in a five-party system?', accessed at http://www.telegraph.co.uk/news/politics/11153469/Open-thread-Can-British-politics-survive-in-a-five-party-system.html on 01/03/2016.
7. Caroline Lucas (@CarolineLucas). 'Taking legal advice over Green exclusion from TV debates. Apparently "messy" to have too many candidates. Democracy IS messy - sort it out!' https://twitter.com/CarolineLucas/status/521653724729835520?ref_src=twsrc%5Etfw. 13 October 2014. 6:28 am. Tweet.

8. Meadwell, R. (2014), 'Include the Green Party in the TV Leaders' Debates ahead of the 2015 General Election', accessed at https://www.change.org/p/bbc-itv-channel-4-sky-include-the-green-party-in-the-tv-leaders-debates-ahead-of-the-2015-general-election on 29/02/2016.
9. Griggs, I. (2015), 'Green Party mocks male-dominated debates with new campaign poster', accessed at http://www.prweek.com/article/1329926/green-party-mocks-male-dominated-debates-new-campaign-poster on 01/03/2016.
10. Wintour, P. (2014), 'Four-fifths of public want Green party in TV leaders' debates – poll', accessed at http://www.theguardian.com/politics/2014/dec/17/poll-green-party-leaders-election-debates on 01/03/2016.
11. See party likeability scores in 2014–2017 British Election Study.
12. The Guardian (2014), 'Greens ahead of Liberal Democrats in YouGov poll', accessed at http://www.theguardian.com/politics/2014/oct/30/greens-ahead-liberal-democrats-yougov-poll-bbc-tv-leader-debate on 01/03/2016.
13. BBC (2014), 'BBC response to letter from Green Party regarding next year's proposed election debates', accessed at http://www.bbc.co.uk/mediacentre/statements/green-party-letter on 01/03/2016.
14. Mason, R. (2014), 'We're like you: Labour pitch for Green vote in bid to quell revolt on the left', accessed at http://www.theguardian.com/politics/2014/nov/16/labour-ed-miliband-green-vote-pitch-brighton on 01/03/2016.
15. BBC (2015), 'Greens are 'not a major party', suggests Ofcom', accessed at http://www.bbc.co.uk/news/uk-politics-30727083 on 01/03/2016.
16. Morris, N. (2015), 'Cameron: If Greens aren't on TV debates, I won't be either', accessed at http://www.independent.co.uk/news/uk/politics/greens-not-a-major-party-rules-ofcom-9965215.html on 01/03/2016.
17. Harris, J. (2015), 'The Green surge: is this the party that will decide the election?', accessed at http://www.theguardian.com/politics/2015/jan/21/green-surge-party-that-will-decide-election on 01/03/2016.
18. T. Bale, P. Webb & M. Poletti (2015), ESRC Party Members Project (PMP), UK Party Membership Survey 2015, Round 1.
19. A simpler version of this analysis was first carried out in a blog post: Poletti, M. and Dennison, J. (2016), 'How did the Green Surge change the membership of the Green Party?', accessible at http://blogs.lse.ac.uk/politicsandpolicy/the-green-surge-and-how-it-changed-the-membership-of-the-party/ on 07/03/2016.
20. GPEW annual accounts are available from the Electoral Commission, accessed at http://www.electoralcommission.org.uk/ on 14/03/2016. The figure for 2015 is approximate and based on the party's increase in membership in that year.

21. Cowburn, A. (2015), 'Fashion designer Vivienne Westwood to donate £300,000 to the Green Party', accessed at http://www.newstatesman.com/politics/2015/01/fashion-designer-vivienne-westwood-donate-300000-green-party on 14/03/2016.
22. Mendick, R. (2015), 'Vivienne Westwood defrocked by Greens over 'tax avoidance', accessed at http://www.telegraph.co.uk/news/politics/green-party/11487630/Vivienne-Westwood-defrocked-by-Greens-over-tax-avoidance.html on 16/03/2015.
23. Spending data available from the Electoral Commission, accessed at http://search.electoralcommission.org.uk/Search/ on 03/03/2016.

Bibliography

Bale, T., Webb, P. and Poletti, M. (2015), ESRC Party Members Project (PMP), UK Party Membership Survey 2015, Round 1

Dennison, J. (2015) 'The Other Insurgency? The Greens and the Election' in *Parliamentary Affairs*, 68 (suppl 1), 188–205

Evans, G. and Mellon, J. (2015), 'Working class votes and Conservative losses: solving the UKIP puzzle' in *Parliamentary Affairs*, 69 (2), 646–479

Rüdig, W. (2015), *Green Party Membership Survey 2015: Some Preliminary Results*, accessed at https://my.greenparty.org.uk/sites/my.greenparty.org.uk/files/GPEW%20mem%20survey%20Interim%20Report%20July2015-v2.pdf on 03/05/2016

Sides, J. and Vavreck, L. (2013), *The Gamble: Choice and Chance in the 2012 Presidential Election*, Princeton: Princeton University Press.

CHAPTER 5

Car Crashes, Campaigning and Partial Decline

Abstract In this chapter, I analyse the Green Party of England and Wales' (GPEW) decline in poll ratings from late January 2014 until the 2015 General Election. I show how, once the Greens were admitted to the television debates, the media's scrutiny of the party's leadership and policies intensified abruptly. Soon after, the party's leadership and competence ratings nosedived as the GPEW was unable to fully make the transition from a minor party, whose primary concerns were internal democracy and ideological conviction, into an established member of the party system, equipped to offer credible and competent leadership and policies to voters under intense media scrutiny. Thereafter, the GPEW adopted a far more risk-averse approach to national campaigning, which centred increasingly on ideology and protest, rather than policies or personality. At the constituency level, the Greens' campaigning varied broadly, according to both the political context and the ambition of the local party. Overall, the Greens' campaigning capacity was far greater than ever before, following the Green Surge, but was undermined by inexperience and the first-past-the-post electoral system.

Keywords Green Party • Natalie Bennett • Leader effects • Campaigning • Constituency elections

J. Dennison, *The Greens in British Politics*,
DOI 10.1007/978-3-319-42673-0_5

From Discovery to Scrutiny

The Green Party of England and Wales's (GPEW) climb in the polls ended abruptly in late January 2015. At the party's peak on 20 January, more than one in ten Britons was planning to vote Green at the upcoming general election. Though the Greens' poll ratings remained stable at around seven per cent over the next month, from late February they started to decline fairly rapidly to their pre-Surge. The party's changes of fortune coincided convincingly with a series of widely criticised television and radio appearances by party leader Natalie Bennett. Journalists, incentivised both by the need to maintain consumer interest and their duty to scrutinise candidates, moved from a 'discovery' phase, in which it had made sense to promote the electoral potential of the Greens, to a 'scrutiny' phase that focused far more on policy. "Once a candidate [in our case, a party] seemed 'serious' enough to pay attention to, that candidate was then subjected to increased scrutiny from both opponents and the news media ... Reporters delved into the candidate's personal history, issue positions, and performance in office ... At times, the candidate him- or herself lent a hand, even unwittingly ... These 'gaffes' only invited further scrutiny" (Sides and Vavreck 2013: 44–45).

On 25 January, just two days after the Greens were admitted onto the televised leaders' debates, Natalie Bennett was 'skewered' in a BBC interview in which she was unable to defend the fiscal logic of her party's spending and taxation plans and her party's radical policies on immigration and defence (Dennison 2015: 195). Bennett recalls how being scrutinised on fiscal specifics had taken her by surprise–"I was expecting to go in and do five minutes on the sofa with the other guests." Instead, Andrew Neil, the interviewer, immediately delved into the party's policies in a manner that resembled little of the convivial tone taken just days earlier, interrupting her an incredible 125 times during the 15-minute interview. More fundamentally, the GPEW leader clearly had little idea of the numbers or viability of her party's often-grandiose policy promises. Bennett linked the obvious change in media tone to her party being admitted to the television debates. "The broadcasters came in and said we were in the debates and that's when, suddenly, everything changed. The media started to treat us very differently without any warning or preparation ... before, we'd been some entertainment and, then, they actually saw us as a threat."

One month later Natalie Bennett would be caught in a similar, far more damaging situation in a national radio interview with broadcaster

LBC. Prior to the interview, Bennett had been suffering from a cold and colleagues had urged her to cancel her appearance. However, the leader ignored their advice and, according to Green insiders, again failed to study the financial specifics of the party's housing policy, which had been released earlier that day. The policy promised to build half a million new homes over the next Parliament–the same amount as had been built in the entire preceding twenty years. When asked how her party would finance the housing policy, Bennett repeatedly coughed, sputtered, paused, mumbled responses and tried to change the subject as she was plainly unable to answer the question. When she did provide figures, they came across as ludicrous, proposing that the total cost of building the new homes would be £2.7 billion. Nick Ferrari, the interviewer, responded, "500,000 new homes, £2.7 billion? What are they made of, plywood?" Powerless to answer, Bennett told Ferrari, "sorry, as you can probably hear, I've got a huge cold." At the party's campaign launch later that day, which was overshadowed by the interview, the GPEW leader apologised to her party's membership for what she described as a 'brain fade'.

Immediately, the interview was picked up by major news channels and newspapers and 'went viral' online. Even Bennett admitted that the interview was "excruciating",[1] while journalists widely panned her performance as a "car crash",[2] "incredibly awkward"[3] and a "disaster".[4] Owen Jones, a left-wing political commentator who might normally be sympathetic towards the Greens' message, tweeted, "unbearably awful interview. Green supporters will be exasperated that a great political opportunity has been trashed."[5] In the 24 hours following the LBC interview, Natalie Bennett was Google's most searched for party leader in the UK– more than all of the other leaders combined.[6] Chris Luffingham, Director of Communications, remembers that the interview "was being touted as the worst political interview of all time, certainly in the top five." One high-profile Green politician lamented that "Natalie didn't manage to actually do what she needed to, or what the Greens needed her to do. And that disastrous interview where she has a brain fade marked a point where actually the Green Surge stopped surging." Whereas the Greens had heartily welcomed the increased media interest in their party over the preceding month, they were now briskly taught that exposure can have its downsides.

No other event is mentioned as much by Green members when reflecting on their 2015 General Election campaign as the LBC interview. Darren Johnson, Green Member of the London Assembly, concluded that "our credibility definitely suffered a blow, and I know from voters coming up to me on the station platform in the morning, saying, 'what the hell was all that interview about? I usually vote Green, but bloody hell.'" Peter Barnett agrees that it "had an enormous effect, to be honest, because from that point onward our credibility really went downhill very fast." One key member of the Greens' national campaign recalls that the interview did not only hint at a lack of credibility, it "waved, and shouted, and jumped up and down saying, 'we are not credible'. I remember getting off the train at Liverpool Street Station, where they have massive digital screens, and Natalie's plastered over all of them. It was at that point I thought, 'Oh, this really is not good. *She's* really not good.'"

Following the LBC interview, Bennett gave other disappointing media performances, with one BBC Radio appearance in early April described by *The Telegraph* as "yet another difficult interview."[7] The 'scrutiny' stage of Sides and Vavreck's 'discovery, scrutiny, and decline' framework was completed as some national newspapers published unsavoury, though thoroughly minor, details from the personal lives of Bennett and her partner, as well as speculating on a rift between the GPEW leader and the party's only MP, Caroline Lucas.[8, 9, 10] By this point, however, the media had shifted its attention elsewhere and the Greens' decline ended with them plateauing at around five per cent in the polls in the month prior to the election. Sides and Vavreck observe, "Having devoted some time to writing about a particular candidate, the media had a natural incentive to move on and find a storyline that was novel and more exciting (2013: 45)." Attention switched from the Greens, whose earlier potential to radically affect the election result had been dashed by their inability to withstand scrutiny, to fresh political events.

Although the media's attention may have moved elsewhere, the damage done to the party is accounted by members and candidates as long lasting. Party strategists had to rethink how to deal with future media performances and how their pledges and commitments, some of which dated back decades, could be best presented. "Where it hit us was in our ability to explain our policies", recalls Darren Hall. One strategist put it more brusquely: "after that event I could no longer plan … and I had to take this leader, who is now badly emotionally and psychologically scarred by this experience and make sure that we don't have that again on national TV … she would say to anybody who was listening that the LBC thing didn't affect her at all … but it did, it really did." Against this background, plans to use Bennett as a spokeswoman for the party had to be rethought including, ironically, in the very televised debates that had sparked the Green Surge and increased press attention of the party.

Green Party parliamentary candidates also recall having to defend their leader while campaigning right up until the general election. The Greens' candidate for Totnes, Gill Coombs, remembers that at her stall voters "would say 'oh, your leader' and roll their eyes." Helen Geake, candidate for Bury St Edmonds, mentions that "I did get adverse comments about Natalie Bennett's media performance", while Huddersfield candidate Andrew Cooper, like many other candidates, was keen to balance out the negatives of Bennett's interview with other positives she brought. He argues that "she was a positive force for good in the campaign and worked seemingly tirelessly getting round the target constituencies and drawing big crowds so you've got to look at the whole package but the interview was certainly brought up on the doorstep as a negative."

The Television Debates

The first televised leaders' debate was held on 2 April and included seven party leaders. Privately, the Greens were irritated that they had to share a stage with the SNP and Plaid Cymru. One member of the party's team said, "we were no longer the only woman on the panel presenting an anti-austerity message. What we say, and what they say, isn't really all that different (Cowley and Kavanagh 2015: 157)." Of even more concern was ensuring that their party leader avoided any particularly bad blunders. One party insider recalls, "in our debate preparation, which now went into kind of overdrive, our objective was to rebuild Natalie, so that she was psychologically strong enough to be able to do it and give her the tools to be able to cope with that. And as much as it was about debate prep, it was kind of a duty of care process, in making sure that she felt safe and supported." The approach to the debates, by far the party's best opportunity for coverage in its history, was by this point one of resignation to minimising damage. The party ran only two full debate rehearsals and, despite filming them both, decided not to watch them for fear of doing more harm to Bennett's confidence (Cowley and Kavanagh 2015: 158).

In the seven leaders' debate, Bennett argued for maintaining public spending on social services and health, higher taxes, EU freedom of movement and immigration, as well as lamenting Britain's record in admitting Syrian refugees. However, her performance was fairly understated. Shortly afterwards, a poll showed that five per cent of voters thought that Bennett performed best in the debate, the second lowest leader and far behind SNP leader Nicola Sturgeon.[11] The same poll showed that Bennett's worst topic in the debate was the economy, at three per cent, and her best was immigration, at seven per cent. Overall, the Greens were unable to take ownership over any issue.

Two weeks later, Bennett took part in a second debate that did not include either David Cameron or Nick Clegg and was thus dubbed the opposition leaders' debate. Bennett's most memorable lines focused on Labour's policy of austerity and a rejection of UKIP's anti-immigration rhetoric. "What we need is a much stronger alternative to the Tories, and that's not what Labour are offering", said Bennett, before going on to criticise Farage, "who wants to utterly demonise those migrants ... I want to celebrate the contribution of migrants to Britain and I think we should all be doing that." Despite the fewer competitors, polls again showed that only five per cent of viewers thought Bennett performed best, with 22 per cent thinking she was the worst participant.[12] Bennett's best topic was deemed to be housing, with 15 per cent ranking her as the best, while her worst was the debt and deficit. Overall, the viewers' impression of Bennett was relatively poor and better only than Leanne Wood, whose Welsh nationalists stood candidates in just five per cent of Britain's seats.

An especially memorable moment followed the debate, when Natalie Bennett, Leanne Wood and Nicola Sturgeon embraced on stage, confirming both their anti-austerity alliance and the clear contrast that they wished to convey between their female-led parties and Miliband's Labour and Farage's UKIP. The hug would be considered one of the highlights of the campaign, particularly to those well versed in Britain's adversarial political culture. In reality the three parties, mostly competing in separate constituencies, had little to gain from attacking each other and everything to gain from coordinating. Sturgeon, whose main political rival in Scotland was Labour, advised the English electorate to vote for the Greens.[13] The hug seemed to resonate with voters. One voter told a Green candidate how "that group of women impressed me and were clearly the best ones, and so I'm going to vote Green." Keith Taylor, MEP for the South East, argues, "the solidarity of the three women I think was the best thing about those broadcasts, as far as the Greens were concerned." Jean Lambert, MEP for London, concluded that following the debates "we were seen as part of the political fabric." Inclusion in the debates confirmed the Greens' place in Britain's refigured party system but their own risk-aversion, following Bennett's difficult interviews, coupled with the competition they faced for attention by the two left-libertarian national party leaders meant that the Greens could not fully capitalise on their historic opportunity.

Bennett as a Leader

Though Greens tended to evaluate Bennett's media performances negatively, many praised her work in internally managing the party and enthusing its members. "The work Natalie did shouldn't be forgotten when explaining the Green Surge", says Judy Maciejowska, former GPEW Regional Development Manager, "going to local meetings … helping local parties grow and advising them – she did a splendid job on that. She came to the South West during the European campaign so many times." Sam Riches, GPEx Policy Coordinator, was also glowing in reference to Bennett: "I would say, overall as leader, I think Natalie's done an absolutely fantastic job." Gill Coombs similarly says, "Bennett quietly in her own kind of workhorse, very steady way, did a fantastic job of building up membership particularly amongst young people." Bennett was roundly commended for her engagement with local Green parties across the country.

Others were less positive, particularly about their leader's ability to front the national campaign of what was no longer an entirely minor party. One member of staff concluded that "she was out of her depth during the election period … she's too excitable" with another stating "what she's not good at, she's never been good at, is preparing. She's not a detailed person at all." One participant in the national campaign contrasted her great ability to communicate and enthuse people internally with her inability to engage the electorate. "She was just naïve. I've got plenty of time for Natalie. She was a core element in the Green Surge, getting out and meeting so many local parties, local people, the work she did there was great and that type of leadership was fantastic. But as a public face for the party, it's been catastrophic. Her strategic reasoning was lacking." One long-term high-profile Green concludes, "Natalie Bennett did a great job leading us to the Green Surge. However, I think she may have hit a bit of a ceiling, with her weak showings on LBC etc. I think in the end that we need another leader if we are to break through to having more than one MP."

The GPEW leader's decision to stand in an unwinnable constituency was repeatedly criticised. "When Natalie Bennett decided to run in Camden rather than Norwich she pretty much single-handedly wrecked our chances of getting a second MP. She would have, without a doubt, been elected in Norwich … if I had a couple of beers I'd be less polite about what I thought of that decision." Green members continued to criticise their leader's decision to stand in north London on the party's message boards after the election, particularly after it emerged that she spent double the amount of the winning Labour candidate on campaigning, only to finish in third place.[14] "I can't help think that Natalie Bennett spending £40k on a non-target seat which we all knew we never had a hope of winning was a ridiculous vanity project", wrote Matt Townsend, a member of the Norwich Green Party.[15] The GPEW leader's strategic and public speaking skills were the most common points of criticism from members in interviews.

Whereas members' assessments were divided, voters assessed Natalie Bennett and her campaign in largely negative terms. Her likeability amongst the public remained stable at 3.5 on a 0–10 scale from late February 2015 until June 2015 (British Election Study 2014–2017). This score put her in practically the joint bottom position amongst party leaders in England, slightly ahead of Nigel Farage at 3.4, but behind Ed Miliband at 3.8, Nick Clegg at 4 and David Cameron at 4.3. One positive statistic from the campaign was that the public became more aware of Bennett as the election approached–the percentage of people responding 'don't know' when asked to give the GPEW leader a likeability score fell from 39 per cent in February-March to 22 per cent in April–May to 19 per cent after the election.[16] However, even Bennett's likeability score amongst those voting for her party was the joint lowest of any leader at 6.4, tied with Ed Miliband but behind Nick Clegg at 6.8, David Cameron at 7.7 and Nigel Farage at 7.8. Moreover, as shown in Fig. 5.1, besides Natalie Bennett's personal likeability score, voters also ranked her campaign as the worst of any leader.

Despite the criticisms from some colleagues and poor assessment by voters, the fact remains that Natalie Bennett presided over the most successful period of the GPEW's history. Her mistakes and shortcomings mirrored the challenges of a party whose primary concern suddenly switched from internal party politics to external media scrutiny and who lacked the experience to successfully make that transition. As the GPEW leader herself admits, during this scrutiny period 'in the middle of it all, all I was thinking was to just survive the next thing.' Bennett, by all accounts, has been excellent at energising and, in an informal way, coordinating what remains a comparatively bottom-up, decentralised party. However, as interviews with party insiders and candidates show, poor media performances sapped confidence inside the party. Decision-makers became introspective, risk-averse and, ultimately, timid just before the election and

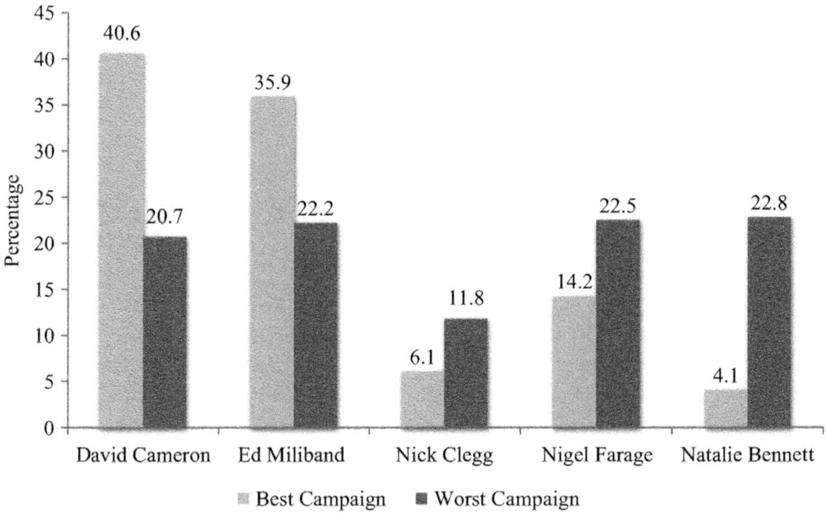

Fig. 5.1 Which party leader has had the best and worst campaign? (Source: British Election Study 2015)

when much of their appeal had rested on their 'exciting', insurgent profile. Dealing with negative public reaction to Bennett's media performance disrupted and distracted the party's campaigning efforts. The impact of Bennett's media performances with the electorate is confirmed both by the party's own candidates, who repeatedly report having to deal with negative comments about their leader while campaigning, and in the negative survey responses to the GPEW leader's campaign.

From Personality to Policies

Though Natalie Bennett had the unfortunate role of party figurehead during the media's most intensive scrutiny of the party, journalists criticised the GPEW's policies just as much as they panned the party's leader. Within the space of four days, just before and after the GPEW was admitted to the television debates, major publications such as *This Week*, *The Independent*, *The Financial Times* and *The Spectator*, which all previously had heralded the 'UKIP of the Left', dismissed the Greens' policies as "a joke", "daft", "completely bonkers" and befitting a "hippie gap year" (Dennison 2015: 194). Indeed, between February and March, numerous newspaper articles simply listed Green policies–such as zero or negative economic growth, decriminalising membership of terrorist organisations and progressive removal of immigration controls–which they considered to be "incoherent, dangerous and unfit for even a junior coalition partner."[17] These policies were not taken from the party's manifesto, which would not be launched until 14 April, but instead from the Greens' *Policies for a Sustainable Society* (*PSS*)– a lengthy, collection of policies cumulatively voted for at party conferences over the previous forty years. Though the document, which the party put into the public realm as a point of principle, had been a cornerstone of the GPEW's democratic internal institutions, under media scrutiny it repeatedly gave cause for embarrassment. *The Financial Times* wrote, "if you attended a hundred bohemian dinner parties, scribbled down every cockamamie idea you overheard and collated them into an anthology, it would not be a million miles from the Green Party's policy programme."[18]

The GPEW's Policy Committee had gone through the document to weed out potentially embarrassing passages but what Green members considered controversial was quite different to what journalists did. Sam Riches, GPEx Policy Coordinator, reflects that "if you're looking to be a trouble making journalist, you'll read it in a completely different way from a nice fluffy members." Realising how damaging *Policies for a Sustainable Society* could be for their credibility, the Greens belatedly edited the online version of the document, altering its description from "all the policies agreed at successive Green Party conferences" to an "organic and evolving document", with "policy chapters" renamed as "long term goals."[19] However, changes in semantics were unable to placate journalists, not least because Green spokespeople had routinely described it as containing their policies in the past. The document was "fine when there were 3,000 members and nobody took any notice of us but it isn't fine anymore", says Sam Riches, "I suggested that we should remove it and several other people have as well but 'No. Transparency is everything'."

Often policies in the *PSS* had been voted through by very small numbers of conference attendees, sometimes many years earlier. Brian Heatley, former GPEx Policy Coordinator, laments, "Conference passes things quite easily … and is indulgent of things put before it." The Greens, given the membership and funds of an established party overnight, were still caught up in the internal procedures of a minor party, rather than proving themselves to the electorate as a credible junior coalition partner or alternative opposition. As Rupert Read, leading Green and 2015 candidate for

Cambridge, says, "too much time is taken up within the party agonising over getting our own structures right – we need to project our message more forcefully to the public." Unfortunately for the Greens, the media fallout from the *Policies for Sustainable Society* document would eventually overshadow the party's election manifesto.

The party had been working on its election manifesto since setting up its Manifesto Working Group in the summer of 2014. As had been the case in 2010, Andrew Dobson, a Professor in Politics at Keele University, and Brian Heatley, a former senior civil servant, were selected to write the manifesto. Both had worked together at the environmentalist think tank *Green House*. The first task for the co-authors was to decide on the party's approach to the fiscal deficit and what they considered to be acceptable taxation levels. This would then have to be agreed with the Manifesto Working Group, which included key national campaign figures, elected officials and representatives of Green councillors. As Brian Heatley remembers, this was crucial because of the party's reputation for fiscal irresponsibility: "The Green Party is notorious. We have a huge list of potential spending commitments and in a sense the question I asked the politicians was 'how much do you feel comfortable raising tax by?'" The party agreed that they would pledge to shrink the fiscal deficit, though not entirely, over the course of the Parliament *and* that they would increase public spending from 40 per cent of GDP to 45 per cent,[20] a position that would be financed by increased tax revenues.[21]

With the basic financial parameters in place, the manifesto authors turned towards deciding on a central theme around which to weave policy promises. The Manifesto Working Group decided to stick to the party's recently adopted slogan 'For the Common Good', which would eventually be the manifesto's title. Mark Cridge, GPEx Management Coordinator and the party's marketing guru, devised the slogan and reflects that "it's not perfect but it recognised the shift to the left in the party and also gave a sense of purpose beyond … talking about planet or climate."

The manifesto authors also had to deal with the internally divisive topic of a universal citizens' income. In Spring 2014, the GPEW conference had passed a motion to make 'citizens' income' an official party policy, promising every citizen at least £80 per week from the state regardless of circumstances. The conference then took the unusual step of passing a motion to explicitly ensure that the policy would appear in the party's forthcoming general election manifesto. Almost immediately, a divide opened up at the top of the party between Natalie Bennett, who was very much in favour of the policy, and other leading Greens, particularly parliamentary candidates including Caroline Lucas, who were anxious of a 'something-for-nothing' image that might harm the party's credibility on the doorstep. The manifesto authors were forced to produce two drafts, one including the policy and one without it.

This split continued until Bennett's infamous interviews, when she was unable to financially defend the policy. The Manifesto Working Group took the unilateral decision to drop the policy from the manifesto in spite of the supposedly binding Conference motion. As a final compromise, the party published a 'consultation' on citizens' income to coincide with the release of their manifesto. Shahrar Ali, Deputy Leader and an advocate of the policy, lamented the party's flip-flop on the issue: "we ended up with something of a fudge which is that we're advocating it but we don't have the complete costings ... I felt that because of a few bad reactions, hostile media and all the rest of it, we understated our commitment to it. And I think that's a very bad sign for any party."

Adding to these difficulties was the emerging division over the issue of immigration within the Manifesto Working Group. On the one hand, some argued that it was ideologically imperative for the Greens to stick to a purely 'open doors' policy, with others pushing for the use of the word 'control' somewhere in the manifesto. As was the case with citizen's income, the latter group were mostly parliamentary candidates anxious about the possibility of difficult conversations with voters. Ultimately, the co-authors inserted the blunt phrase "some controls on immigration will be needed for the foreseeable future; for now, we reject an open doors approach."[22]

Overall, the authors of the manifesto felt that, though it was better than previous attempts, there was still room for improvement. "We wound up with a manifesto that was much too long and much too detailed", summarises Heatley, "partly that means your candidates cannot master it, partly there are inevitably more hostages to fortune." However, "it was a lot better this time" than in 2010.

The exacting media scrutiny of the party's leader and backdated policies convinced the party to launch their manifesto with a whimper rather than a bang. Indeed, just fourteen minutes after arriving to launch the manifesto, both Natalie Bennett and Caroline Lucas left for appointments elsewhere, leaving Brian Heatley to field questions. The manifesto's key promises–protect and increase public services for children and pensioners, expand public sector jobs, build 500,000 homes, create one million jobs that pay a 'living wage', abolish university tuition fees, nationalise rail and subsidise rail prices and invest in green sources of energy–were eye-catching and all required increases in public spending. To match the spending promises, the party outlined projections of increased revenues via a new 'wealth tax', a 'Robin Hood tax', clamping down on tax evasion, new aviation and fuel taxes and an increased corporation tax, which, amongst other measures, would raise an additional £200 billion by 2020–more than ten per cent of the UK's entire gross domestic product. When asked about the new taxes Brian Heatley admitted to the press that he could not be sure about the proposed revenues because many had not been tried before but they would work "up to a point." "A bit like the Green Party", quipped *The Guardian*.[23]

During the 2015 election campaign, the GPEW was unable to change the public's perception that the party was economically 'illiterate'. Caroline Lucas states, "it almost doesn't matter what a Green Party politician says about the economy, because as soon as it comes out the math is dismissed. We are not seen as credible on the economy." This perception was underlined by the lack of confidence that party members had in discussing fiscal issues. "In the senior parts of the party, with one or two exceptions, they aren't really comfortable talking about numbers", says Brian Heatley.

The perception of economic illiteracy gave voters who sympathised with the Greens' messages of environmentalism and anti-austerity doubts about whether the Greens could translate their principles into effective policies. Tom Chance, Green Coordinator in the Greater London Assembly, remembers voters telling him "well, what you're saying is all fine, well and good, but it doesn't really stack up, does it?" or "I was very disappointed that you couldn't actually deliver on this stuff." He goes on to say that those who were drawn to the Greens' 'big ideas' during the TV debates controversy turned away from the party after they "got the sense that we couldn't really explain what we were trying to do. Our maths didn't really add up. It wasn't really credible and so it was a protest vote. It was a vote for a nice idea, but it wasn't a vote for a serious principled programme."

The pesky need to justify their long list of backdated policies, a lack of confidence in their own fiscal convictions and a dismal manifesto launch convinced the Greens to rely on appeals of principle and protest rather than policy. When Labour started selling coffee mugs emblazoned with each of their five policy slogans, the mug that stated 'Controls on immigration' garnered controversy and ridicule. The Greens quickly responded by producing their own mug with the slogan 'Standing up for migrants', one of the party's notable outright successes at the national level during the election campaign.

The other success of the national campaign, certainly in terms of gaining visibility, was the GPEW's party election broadcast, entitled 'Change the Tune', which was viewed nearly 900,000 times on YouTube, more than all of the other parties' broadcasts combined. The broadcast portrayed the leaders of the four other parties as a 1990s boy band singing in a 'party political harmony' about their consensus on 'neo-liberal' economics, austerity, anti-immigration sentiment and lax attitudes to corporate greed. It was also bookended by a narrator espousing the Greens' principles and imploring viewers to vote ideologically by "voting true, not tactical". Like in other GPEW campaign publications, the broadcast argued that "the only wasted vote is a vote you don't believe in" and portrayed the Greens as the genuine opposite to the establishment. Mark Cridge, who worked on the broadcast, says, "the election broadcast was really high risk, really fun. We intentionally used humour to soften the image of the party to help people recognise that these issues are serious but we do have a sense of perspective – it's not all po-faced. In both 2014 and 2015 we were trying to say, 'look guys they're all the same. UKIP is trying to play themselves as outsiders but honestly they're all the same'." Though one member complained that it was "dreadful" or was even "offended" by it, the impressive publicity that the broadcast directed to the party qualified it as a success to central party members. By this point, it was clear to party insiders that the least risky, most successful campaigning tactics involved principle and protest, not policy.

This approach was reflected in the party's campaign billboard–a long list of reasons to vote for the GPEW, which was partially based on the 'Choose Life' monologue from the 1990s film *Trainspotting* and was unveiled by Caroline Lucas and Natalie Bennett on the day before the party's manifesto launch. The text read "Vote big. Vote brave. Vote for what you believe in. Vote it off your chest. Vote because you're not your parents. Vote because the planet can't. Vote because UKIP will. Vote while we can still fix this. Vote people into half a million affordable homes. Vote doctors back into hospitals. Vote the economy back to health. Vote to stand with us. Vote for the common good. Vote Green." The elaborate message combined the party's ideological and anti-establishment values, though was light on policy.

When discussing policy, the party stuck to a few key promises. Natalie Bennett states that there were "three simple messages that we just kept banging on and on about until people heard – making the minimum wage a living wage, renationalising the railways, and a publicly owned and publicly-run NHS." All of which were historically popular, classically left-wing policies. More broadly, the Greens framed themselves as anti-austerity. Caroline Lucas says that, rather than this election being about policy, "it was more generally about not compromising the message, particularly on austerity." The party also aimed to signal to the public that they were unwilling to go along with the more anti-immigration trends in British politics. "The immigration thing was more just about helping to create in people's minds this impression that a principled party is willing to stand against the drift in the mainstream political and media world", says Tom Chance. Caroline Lucas makes clear that there was a strategic decision to say to voters, "if you don't like the three main parties, you don't have to vote for UKIP, there is a party that's on the left but has the same kind of vigour as UKIP but stands for a very, very different way forward ... there was a conscious effort to be taking that space."

Greens also couched their campaign messaging in terms of activism, rather than policy specifics. Caroline Lucas affirms, "as political parties, we over-play the importance of policy details. For most people, it's much more about how they feel about you, and if they feel that you're standing up for them and if they see you on the picket lines." Lucas was not alone amongst leading Greens in seeing policy as not a key part of their party's role. Brian Heatley, despite writing the manifesto, argues that policy is not the Greens' goal; instead it is "about widening the moral vision" of society. One result of a lack of emphasis on policy was that voters were left unaware of the party's programme. Tom Chance recalls, "we've done focus groups to ask people what they think about what Green Party policies are. Their understanding of us is a lot more vague than we'd hoped."

Following confidence-sapping setbacks, the GPEW deemphasised personality and policy in their campaign and, instead, focussed on messages of principle and protest. In doing so, the party inadvertently framed themselves as a protest vote–a luxury that left-wing voters could ill afford in the tight 2015 electoral race for 10 Downing Street. Previous studies have shown that voters are less likely to vote for third or fourth parties in times of close electoral competition "even if they are dissatisfied with their normal party's policies or behaviour" (Kang 2004: 81; see also Johnston 1984). Furthermore, only a small section of the British electorate were receptive to the Greens' ideological message in its purest form. Just 6.3 per cent of the electorate believed both that measures to protect the environment 'have not gone *nearly* far enough' and that cuts to public spending 'have gone *much* too far'. By contrast, an additional 23.8 per cent of the electorate agreed with the more moderate statements that measures to protect the environment 'have not gone far enough' and that cuts to public spending 'have gone too far'. Supporters of UKIP's core ideological message, stated in its most extreme form, were more numerous–22 per cent of the electorate agreed that, with regard to the European Union, Britain should *entirely* 'protect its independence' and that immigration should be 'decreased *a lot*' (British Election Study 2014–2017).[24]

Constituency Campaigns

Although the GPEW's national campaign failed to be as forceful as some had hoped it would be during the heady days of the Green Surge, the party's constituency campaigns varied in intensity, approach and competition significantly. The retention of the Brighton Pavilion seat was the party's primary political objective. Just prior to the Green Surge, however, a constituency poll had put the Greens at 32 per cent, one point behind Labour.[25] Labour had selected a leftist candidate, Purna Sen, a British Asian long-term resident of Brighton with a career in human rights–working for Amnesty International and Justice for Gay Africans–who stood on a platform of rail renationalisation, anti-nuclear energy and pro-immigration and had, in 2003, marched against the War in Iraq. The Labour candidate attacked the Greens' zero-growth agenda and their poor record of delivering houses locally, as well as contrasting her approach of change via governance with the Greens' approach of change via protest.[26]

The main charge brought against Lucas was that her party was to blame for Brighton's rubbish strike and, ironically, Brighton and Hove Council's incredibly poor record on recycling. Sam Riches remembers, "It was a dirty campaign." In response, the Greens in Brighton focused incessantly on Lucas' record in Westminster. Lucas recalls that her tactic was "very much to stand on my record. Labour was trying to paint me as being a super-councillor, really. The phrase they kept using was 'Caroline's Council' for every time your rubbish wasn't collected, it was Caroline's Council, that was the hashtag that was widely used on Twitter."

Less than three weeks prior to the election, a group of 40 highly prominent figures, such as conservationist Sir David Attenborough, called for Lucas' re-election. The professionalism of her campaign, described by Mark Cridge as "ruthless and committed–not words you usually use with Green

Party members", was noted by multiple Green insiders. The Brighton campaign was effectively run separately from the national campaign and Lucas admits it is "completely true" that the Surge mattered less there than elsewhere. One Green insider remembers that Lucas' team were concerned, rather than pleased, with the expansion of the Greens' national campaign coverage, which "they thought was negatively affecting their campaign. They really had very little trust in national party operations." Ultimately, Lucas' own personality, public profile, record in the House of Commons and reputation for competence would be enough for the Greens to maintain their sole MP, despite the simultaneous loss of control over the council.

Events in Brighton affected the national campaign more than *vice versa*. Not only did the party have to produce a booklet to "dispel the myths of Brighton Council", but the crucial race between two candidates eager to outflank each other as the most left wing and pro-immigration forced the national party to follow suit. Tom Chance states that it was important "to try and present a national image that was helpful to Brighton, and this time around Bristol as well, even if that may create difficulties in other parts of the country. So, councillors in rural areas who had previously seen off Conservative candidates found that quite difficult because the party was developing an image that wasn't a platform that Greens got elected on locally." The arithmetic of the Westminster electoral system forced the GPEW to build its national campaign, which included over 500 seats, around the single, demographically and politically anomalous, seat of Brighton Pavilion.

The next tier of target constituencies after Brighton Pavilion comprised Bristol West and Norwich South. The former ran a far more vigorous and ambitious campaign than the latter. In Bristol, Darren Hall, a polished former civil servant, RAF officer and company director of the Bristol Green Capital Partnership, who had only joined the Green Party in 2014, faced a three-way battle with a Liberal Democrat incumbent and a confident Labour Party. Hall argues that in his constituency the Greens offered an organisation for a distinct ideological group to coalesce around, following their disillusionment with the Liberal Democrats. "A lot of the voters that I gained this time were about values. They were the same people that voted for the Lib Dems against Labour when Blair went in to Iraq." These voters were then up for grabs when the Liberal Democrat incumbent "Stephen Williams failed to stand up for the student vote, the student fees, and fracking." Bristol West was one of the constituencies that gained most from the Green Surge, with the local party increasing in membership by 700 per cent in eight months. Hall recalls, "we went from about 200 to over 2,000 people, making us the biggest party locally. We are bigger than Labour, bigger than Lib Dems … making us the biggest Green Party in the country." The Surge allowed for campaigning events in Bristol West that outshone those of the other parties, with hundreds of followers attending photo opportunities, music events, talks and Green-led forums.

The GPEW benefitted in Bristol West from the city's strong alternative cultural scene, anti-establishment politics and the honour of being the 2015 European Green Capital.[27] However, a left-wing Labour candidate as well as a series of Green missteps would ultimately undermine the Greens' campaign. Mark Cridge remembers that "from the outside I could see Bristol wasn't a well oiled machine in the same way that Brighton was and to win an election you need a well oiled machine. You need to have canvassed the entire constituency at least twice in the preceding six months. You need to have a massive get-out-the-vote operation. You need to have your candidate in place at least 12 months before." Not only did the party not manage to organise itself with a proper campaigning team until early 2015, it was then blighted by a major falling out between the highly autonomous local party and the national party. This rift culminated in Chris Luffingham, Director for Communications, being banned from entering the constituency and the local party refusing to share its data or relinquish any control over the local campaign.

In the party's other target constituency, Norwich South, the party campaigned with less drive than in 2010 when candidate Adrian Ramsay, often credited with building the local party, had secured 15 per cent of the vote. The 2015 candidate, Lesley Grahame, an eco-socialist, member of Green Left and local nurse, oversaw a party that, by Green Surge standards, saw modest growth from 200 to 700 members and made less of an impression than in Bristol West. Unlike in the GPEW's top two constituencies, the campaign in Norwich was unable to frame the Greens as a dynamic, progressive option that might offer pragmatic solutions. Labour again selected a far-left candidate–a self-described socialist, who opposed TTIP, Trident and austerity, with a trade union and army background who described his political hero as Tony Benn.[28] In Norwich South, better than anywhere, Labour outmanoeuvred the Greens in the constituency campaign by mixing left-wing politics that were similar to those of the Greens with practical realities. By contrast, the GPEW candidate was unable to secure the local profile that the Greens had elsewhere.[29]

Outside of the three key targets seats, the constituency campaigns of the GPEW were not run with a view to winning the seat. As was the case in Bristol West, numerous candidates had only agreed to stand for the party a few months before the election, often having been attracted to the party very recently. Dee Searle, candidate for Tottenham, laments that "I was selected in late January ... if we'd had a few more months, so another three months, we could have possibly come second." Gill Coombs, in Totnes, had joined the party in 2013 and agreed to stand only after it appeared that the party would not be able to put forward a candidate. Coombs admits that "I didn't really know what I was doing because I was new to politics, I made a lot of it up as I went along." Davy Jones, in Brighton Kemptown, started even later: "I was selected in January 2015 and began working in April 2015."

In constituencies such as Lancaster and Fleetwood, a Conservative-Labour marginal, the Greens' campaign was overshadowed by the battle between the major parties. Sam Riches, a former Green councillor in the area, says, "there was such a strong drive of, 'we've got to get Labour back in and Cat Smith.' What they did was to pile their resources into Lancaster, desperately trying to get the Green vote to elect the Labour MP. So, for example, she's anti-fracking, and various other things, which are completely against Labour Party policy but are in line with the Greens." The combination of a marginal seat and an organised Labour Party with a leftist candidate tended to lessen the visibility of the Greens' campaign.

However, even in their safe seats Labour often aped the messaging of the Greens. In Hackney South and Shoreditch, Green candidate Charlotte George says, "the Labour Party's strategy was to ... suggest that they were very comfortable with the [Greens'] ideas", which George says were roundly applauded at debates. In urban seats the Greens found greater success using bottom-up tactics, despite facing the Labour party machine. Like in Bristol West, the Hackney South and Shoreditch Greens offered social activities such as weekly pub nights and family-friendly afternoons to mobilise new members, which then translated into far greater campaigning capabilities.

In Tottenham, another Labour safe seat in London, the Greens experienced similar new-found capabilities thanks to the Green Surge. "People wanted to do things, they wanted to help out, giving out leaflets, to hand out fliers at stations", states candidate Dee Searle. She also notes that, whereas the local party had originally planned to distribute 1,000 postcards to households, "We had all these young people coming, our new members, saying 'Can I give out some postcards?' So in total, it was something like 50,000 postcards that we distributed." Jonathan Bartley, in Streatham, where the Labour incumbent received over 50 per cent of the votes, says, "we set ourselves some goals of using leafleting to introduce new members and engage them, and delivered around 250,000 pieces of literature during the campaign, which was more than anywhere else in London. We also had a big emphasis on social events. We organised a fundraising gig, a film screening, as well as speaker dinners, in order to help people to meet each other and become more in involved."

Some candidates also mention that the Surge presented a challenge that was most keenly felt by local parties. Rupert Read, candidate in Cambridge, remembers that "it was difficult for the party infrastructure to adapt so quickly to having such a vast increase in support; we did incredibly well, under the circumstances. In the 12 months prior to January 2015 we quintupled our membership in Cambridge. This wave of support led to us significantly expanding our operation." The GPEW candidate for Manchester Gorton says of the Surge, "in some ways it gave us more work to do! We were very keen to welcome the new members and draw them in to local activities, so we spent quite a lot of time and energy trying to do that. A good number did get very involved though, so that initial effort was more than paid back."

On policy, the Green candidates report greatly varying experiences. Charlotte George states that, out of the thousands of doors that she knocked on, "I reckon I had four, five people ask me about policy over the three months of door knocking, going out pretty much every week. Hardly anyone." On the other hand, Laura Bannister argues that "the manifesto was the star of the show" and that, regarding the section on costings, "I took to carrying a print out of that chapter around so that whenever feasibility or cost questions came up I could give people real information." Similarly, Helen Geake, candidate in Bury St. Edmonds, states, "when they said, 'but how will you ever fund them?', the costings section at the back of the manifesto was absolutely vital."

One issue that the Greens were unequivocal about was the damaging effect of the first-past-the-post system on their campaign. Davy Jones met "hundreds of people on the doorstep saying that they supported the Greens, I was the best candidate, but they were voting Labour 'to keep the Tory out.'" Charlotte George also recalls voters who were open to her ideas saying, "I don't want to let the Tories in." Less than half of those who, in March 2015, said that they identified most closely with the Greens actually voted for the Greens, with 25 per cent opting for the Labour and 9 per cent for the Liberal Democrats (British Election Study 2014–2017). Natalie Bennett remembers that on the day of the election "people were coming up to me and asking for selfies and just hugging me ... I started asking people how they voted. And they'd say 'you're wonderful! Great!' ... but they'd either say or it was painfully obvious. They voted Labour."

Notes

1. Prince, R. (2015), 'Green Party's Natalie Bennett gives 'excruciating' radio interview', accessed at http://www.telegraph.co.uk/news/politics/green-party/11431756/Green-Partys-Natalie-Bennett-gives-excruciating-radio-interview.html on 03/03/2016.
2. Holehouse, M. (2015), 'Natalie Bennett suffers car crash interview on BBC Radio 4 Today programme', accessed at http://www.telegraph.co.uk/news/politics/green-party/11518984/Natalie-Bennett-suffers-car-crash-interview-on-BBC-Radio-4-Today-programme.html on 03/03/2016.
3. LBC (2015), 'Incredibly Awkward Interview with Natalie Bennett', accessed at http://www.lbc.co.uk/incredibly-awkward-interview-with-natalie-bennett-105384 on 03/03/2016.
4. Thompson, B. and Aglionby, J. (2015), 'Natalie Bennett interview disaster mars Greens' UK election launch', accessed at http://www.ft.com/cms/s/0/512598a0-bc12-11e4-a6d7-00144feab7de.html#axzz42zrLF81h on 03/03/2016.
5. Prince, R. (2015), 'Green Party's Natalie Bennett gives 'excruciating' radio interview', accessed at http://www.telegraph.co.uk/news/politics/green-party/11431756/Green-Partys-Natalie-Bennett-gives-excruciating-radio-interview.html on 03/03/2016.
6. Accessed at https://www.google.co.uk/trends/ on 03/03/2016.
7. Holehouse, M. (2015), 'Natalie Bennett suffers car crash interview on BBC Radio 4 Today Programme', accessed at http://www.telegraph.co.uk/news/politics/green-party/11518984/Natalie-Bennett-suffers-car-crash-interview-on-BBC-Radio-4-Today-programme.html on 03/03/2016.
8. Moss, V. and Warburton, D. (2015), 'General Election 2015: Green party boss Natalie Bennett faces further embarrassment from boyfriend's X-rated rants', accessed at http://www.mirror.co.uk/news/uk-news/general-election-2015-green-party-5546699 on 03/03/2016.
9. Dathan, M. (2015), 'Natalie Bennett interview: I've lost track of the last time I saw my Dad but it's not because I refuse to fly', accessed at http://www.independent.co.uk/news/uk/politics/generalelection/natalie-bennett-interview-ive-lost-track-of-the-last-time-i-saw-my-dad-but-its-not-because-i-refuse-10194921.html on 03/03/2016.

10. Chakelian, A. (2015), 'The Granola Pact: is there a rift between Natalie Bennett and Caroline Lucas?', accessed at http://www.newstatesman.com/politics/2015/03/granola-pact-there-rift-between-natalie-bennett-and-caroline-lucas on 03/03/2016.
11. YouGov (2015), 'Nicola Sturgeon wins leaders' debate', accessed at https://yougov.co.uk/news/2015/04/02/leaders-debate/on 03/03/2016.
12. Survation (2015), 'BBC Election Debate Reactions Poll', accessed at http://survation.com/wp-content/uploads/2015/04/Post-Debate-Poll-Tables.pdf on 03/03/2016.
13. Simons, N. (2015), 'Nicola Sturgeon Urges English to Vote Green Or 'Progressive' Labour', accessed at http://www.huffingtonpost.co.uk/2015/03/16/nicola-sturgeon-urges-english-to-vote-green-or-progressive-labour_n_6876950.html on 03/03/2016.
14. Osley, R. (2015), 'Revealed: How Green leader Natalie Bennett outspent rivals in failed bid to conquer Holborn and St Pancras', accessed at http://www.camdennewjournal.com/electionexpenses on 03/03/2016.
15. Townsend, M. (2015), 'Natalie Bennett spent £40k on a non-target seat – time for a new leader?', accessed at https://my.greenparty.org.uk/forum/national-forums/general-member-discussion/11361 [members only], on 03/03/2016.
16. However, these results may be due to the learning effects of panel surveys, such as this one (British Election Study, 2014–2017), where a respondent's participation in previous waves biases their response.
17. The Spectator (2015), 'Calling the Green party socialist is an insult to socialist', accessed at http://www.spectator.co.uk/2015/01/calling-the-green-party-socialist-is-an-insult-to-socialists/ on 24/03/2016; The Week (2015), 'Natalie Bennett and the Green manifesto: zero growth, free condoms, no monarchy', accessed at http://www.theweek.co.uk/election-2015/62176/natalie-bennett-and-the-green-manifesto-zero-growth-free-condoms-no-monarchy on 24/03/2016; Holehouse, M. (2015), 'Drugs, brothels, al-Qaeda and the Beyonce Tax: the Green Party plan for Britain', accessed at http://www.telegraph.co.uk/news/politics/green-party/11356354/Drugs-brothels-al-Qaeda-and-the-Beyonce-tax-the-Green-Party-plan-for-Britain.html?WT.mc_id=e_3847864&WT.tsrc=email&etype=frontpage&utm_source=email&utm_medium=Edi_FAM_New_2015_1_20&utm_campaign=3847864 on 24/03/2016.
18. Ganesh, J. (2015), 'Greens contemplate life beyond the fringe', accessed at http://www.ft.com/cms/s/0/529f5f22-a240-11e4-bbb8-00144feab7de.html#axzz43quoJT3C on 24/03/2016.
19. Green Party (2015), 'Green Party Policy', accessed at https://policy.greenparty.org.uk/ on 23/03/2016.

20. The party came to this figure because it was the spending rate in Germany, which made it seem more reasonable.
21. The group had originally intended on financing these commitments by 'monetary reform', a form of quantitative easing in which the government increased expenditure on infrastructure projects rather than buying debt, which had recently been set as party policy by the conference. However, out of fear of looking fiscally irresponsible, the party instead settled on tax increases and planning to leave a one per cent deficit at the end of the Parliament. As Brian Heatley recalls, the decision 'was entirely political. Here's the Green Party. They want to spend a lot more money. How are they going to finance it? They're going to print the money. I don't think anyone seriously thought that that was a good place to be.'
22. Green Party (2015), *For the Common Good: General Election Manifesto 2015*, London: Green Party. Pp. 72.
23. Crace, J. (2015), 'Green party manifesto launch: spending on everything ... but time', accessed at http://www.theguardian.com/politics/2015/apr/14/green-party-manifesto-launch-spending-on-everything-but-time on 03/03/2016.
24. The environmentalism, anti-austerity and immigration measures used five-point scales, while the European integration scale is 10 points, so the *two* most Eurosceptic responses are included for this (9 or 10 on the 0–10 scale).
25. Lord Ashcroft Polls (2015), 'Brighton Pavilion', accessed at http://lordashcroftpolls.com/2015/01/brighton-pavilion/ on 03/03/2016.
26. Wigmore, T. (2015), 'Brighton Pavilion: The Greens are in trouble everywhere', accessed at http://www.newstatesman.com/politics/2015/02/brighton-pavilionthe-greens-are-trouble-everywhere on 03/03/2016.
27. Morris, N. (2015), 'Green Party on the march: From a lost deposit to victory – the revolution sweeping Bristol', accessed at http://www.independent.co.uk/news/uk/politics/green-party-on-the-march-from-a-lost-deposit-to-victory-9880698.html on 03/03/2016.
28. Engel, M. (2015), 'Green party candidate faces uphill slog in Norwich South', accessed at http://www.ft.com/cms/s/0/87366da8-b298-11e4-b234-00144feab7de.html#axzz449gkmsRw on 03/03/2016.
29. London Green Left Blog (2015), 'Interview – Green Party Candidate for the General Election – Lesley Grahame, Norwich South', accessed at http://londongreenleft.blogspot.co.uk/2015/04/interview-green-party-candidate-for.html on 03/03/2016.

Bibliography

Cowley, P. and Kavanagh, D. (2015), *The British General Election of 2015*, Basingstoke: Palgrave Macmillan

Dennison, J. (2015) 'The Other Insurgency? The Greens and the Election' in *Parliamentary Affairs*, 68 (suppl 1), 188–205

Johnston, R. (1984), 'Cracking the Mould: The Changing Geographical Pattern of Voting in England, 1979–1983' in *Area*, 16, 101–8.

Kang, W. T. (2004), 'Protest voting and abstention under plurality rule elections: an alternative public choice approach' in *Journal of Theoretical Politics*, 16(1), 79–102.

Sides, J. and Vavreck, L. (2013), *The Gamble: Choice and Chance in the 2012 Presidential Election*, Princeton: Princeton University Press.

CHAPTER 6

Who Voted Green and Why?

Abstract In this chapter, I switch the focus towards the voters. Using the existing literature on voting for Green parties as a foundation, I compare the socio-demographic and attitudinal profiles of those voting for the Green Party of England and Wales and the Scottish Greens with the profiles of other parties' voters. I then establish what explains their decision to vote Green, finding that environmentalist, anti-austerity, libertarian and protest attitudes have strongly positive effects, while classically left-wing attitudes do not. I then test how these effects vary according to political background, finding that Liberal Democrats moved to the Greens because of their leftist attitudes, while Labour voters switched to the Greens because of their more libertarian views. Finally, I use panel data models to show that the Greens' vote was less subject to leader likeability effects than other parties' vote was, whereas voting Green was more dependent on the effects of perception of party competence than voting for any other party.

Keywords Green party • 2015 general election • Party choice • Voting behaviour • Anti-austerity • Protest • Environmentalism • Panel data

The Results

The Green Party of England and Wales (GPEW) received 1,111,603 votes in 2015– 4.1 of all votes in England and Wales and 4.3 per cent in seats in which they stood a candidate. Despite more than quadrupling their

J. Dennison, *The Greens in British Politics*,
DOI 10.1007/978-3-319-42673-0_6

2010 vote share, the party was left with the same number of seats as it had five years earlier, with Brighton Pavilion remaining their sole constituency. The party finished in second place in four constituencies–Bristol West, the Isle of Wight, Sheffield Central and Manchester Gorton. The Greens were able to save their £500 deposit, which requires gaining five per cent or more of the vote share, in 126 of the 536 seats in which they stood a candidate. Many party members expressed severe disappointment at not being able to increase the number of Green Members of Parliament, although, in reality, the Greens were only competitive in two seats across England and Wales and only received more than ten per cent of the vote in just 18 seats.

The Scottish Greens won 39,205 votes, 1.4 per cent of the total votes in Scotland, double their 2010 performance. In seats in which they stood candidates, the party received an average of 2.6 per cent of the vote. The Scottish Green Party stood candidates in only 31 of a possible 59 constituencies, saving their deposit in just three seats. Their top six performances were all in Edinburgh or Glasgow. The Scottish Greens had calculated that, faced with the first-past-the-post system and the soaring SNP, they should save their resources until the 2016 Scottish Parliament election. The Irish Green Party fared slightly better, securing 3.3 per cent of the vote in the five seats in which they stood a candidate and saving their deposit in two.

To determine who voted Green and why, this chapter uses data from the 2014 to 2017 British Election Study (BES). The BES has covered every UK general election since 1964. In 2015, the study was a collaborative project between the University of Manchester, the University of Nottingham and the University of Oxford. For the 2015 election, the BES included both a face-to-face survey and a (so far) six-wave Internet panel survey. For the purposes of this book, the latter Internet survey is more appropriate for two reasons. The face-to-face survey includes 2,197 respondents and just 66 Green voters, far fewer than the panel survey, which includes 41,837 individuals. These individuals took part in at least one of the panel's six waves–held in (Wave 1) February-March 2014, (2) May-June 2014, (3) September-October 2014, (4) February-March 2015, (5, pre-election) April-May 2015 and (6, post-election) May-June 2015. The panel nature of the Internet study allows us to see how respondents' political attitudes and voting intention changed throughout the panel. Wave six asks the respondents for whom they ultimately voted, with 27,771 giving a response and 1,419 of them voting for the Greens

(1,306 in England and Wales and 113 of 5,118 respondents in Scotland). The study does not include voters in Northern Ireland.

What We Already Know

The emergence of Green parties in advanced democracies in the 1970s and 1980s was greeted by academics with enthusiastic enquiry. The Greens' voters–attracted to the message of environmentalism, feminism, pacifism and grass roots democracy–were quickly interpreted by researchers (Poguntke 1989; Kitschelt 1990) as the strongest adherents to new 'post-material' values, as identified by Inglehart (1977), which prioritised the well-being of the planet and mankind's quality of life over materialist growth, and were drawn to left-libertarian parties, such as the Greens. Poguntke (1989: 59, 68) argued in his study of the German Green Party that 'post-materialist value orientation is the single most important explanatory factor for the emergence of the New Politics and–as a consequence–the Green Party vote' before describing this value orientation as a "commitment to ecology and peace, striving for individual liberties, minority rights and libertarian ideals."

Throughout the 1980s, however, many Green parties became increasingly attached to the traditional left-wing concern of economic inequality and to various degrees saw government redistribution of wealth as the way to increase this (Müller-Rommel 1990). Although studies in the late 1980s were united in their evaluation of the socio-demographic background of Green supporters–young, urban, well educated and white-collar (e.g. Bennulf and Holmberg 1990; Müller-Rommel 1990), as well as non-religious (Poguntke 1989)–comparative analyses showed that the level of post-materialism of Green voters varied from country to country (Müller-Rommel 1985; Kreuzer 1990). Furthermore, Rüdig (1990: 16) warned against underestimating the singular issue of environmentalism as the explanation for why voters were turning to the Greens, asking, "why is it that most social scientists analysing Green parties regard the "ecological" identity of these parties as irrelevant, unimportant or, at best, as marginal? There seems to be a consensus that somehow they cannot be what they appear to be."

Aside from the strong consensus on socio-demographics and environmentalism and the slightly less consistent findings on post-materialism and classic left-wing outlooks, an emerging cultural divide has recently been associated with Green support. In the 21st century, increased global connectedness has led to greater mobility of persons and transfers of powers from nation states to supranational organisations, particularly in the European Union. As discussed in Chap. 2, Western polities have been particularly divided about the appropriate political response to these trends, resulting in an emerging integration-demarcation axis–sometimes called a cultural divide–with Green parties strongly advocating integration (Kriesi et al. 2008). If the emergence of such a divide explains support for the Greens in 2015, we would expect to find evidence of a positive effect of pro-immigration and pro-European attitudes on voting Green. Dolezal (2010) found evidence of a positive effect of pro-immigration–though not pro-European values–on one's likelihood of voting Green in 12 European states.

Unfortunately, Dolezal's work did not include the UK, primarily because of the lack of historic Green support in Britain resulting in an insufficiently large sample of Green voters to reliably analyse. Birch (2009) circumvented this issue by testing the determinants of Green Party affect, showing that youth, education and a favourability towards tax and spend policies all increased sympathy towards the party. Interestingly, though, unlike in Dolezal's analysis, secularism, employment type (divided between public and private sector), favouring individual rights over social order and attitudes to the War in Iraq were not shown to have significant effects.

Following the 2015 election, Dennison (2015) found that Greens in the UK were disproportionately likely to be young, in professional or management jobs, have university degrees (in the humanities), to not be religious and to be students. Green voters were shown to be left wing, though no more than Labour voters, and far more likely than other parties' voters to hold libertarian, environmentalist, pro-migration and pro-EU views. The article also found that Greens were highly dissatisfied with British democracy. While it was safe to conclude that Green voters looked like Lib Dems, thought like Labour and were as dissatisfied as UKIP, the analysis neither included a number of standard social indicators, such as gender or homeownership, nor moved beyond description to explanation of *why* these people voted Green. Clarke et al. (2016) offered an explanatory analysis for Green support, alongside their analyses of support for other British parties. They found the five strongest effects on voting Green were affinity towards the party's leader–Natalie Bennett–Green Party contact, youth, not identifying with Labour and pro-immigration attitudes. They also showed that voting Green can be better explained by socio-demographics than voting for any other party.

Who Votes Green

Based on the literature, I present the socio-demographic and attitudinal profiles of voters of each of the five major English parties, as well as the Scottish Greens and the SNP and the electorate as a whole (see Fig. 6.1). The GPEW attracted the most disproportionately young, female and well-educated voters of any English party. The party's voters were also disproportionately non-White British, though less so than Labour voters.[1] The Scottish Greens–facing competition from the anti-austerity and anti-establishment SNP–attracted voters that were

	Con	Labour	Lib Dem	UKIP	GPEW	Scottish GP	SNP	Electorate
Socio Demographics								
Mean age	49	46	47	51	37	34	45	46
% Under 25	11	14	14	7	30	42	16	13
% Male	49	47	51	54	46	41	51	49
% White British	93	87	92	95	88	92	88	89
% University Degree	25	27	39	14	42	49	26	26
% Homeowner	73	55	65	67	42	33	53	61
% Students	4	5	8	2	14	24	6	5
% No religion	37	45	51	40	65	74	55	45
% Higher professional / Management	20	15	23	13	22	17	14	18
% Lower professional / Intermediate	55	54	54	48	56	31	51	54
% Small employer / Supervisory	14	12	11	19	9	22	14	13
% Routine / Semi-Routine	11	19	11	19	12	30	22	15
Mean household income (000s)	32	26	31	25	28	26	25	28
Attitudes (1-5 unless otherwise stated: 1=disagree, 3=neither, 5=agree)								
Left-right self placement (0-10)	7.0	3.4	4.6	6.3	2.9	2.5	3.4	5.1
Govt should redistribute incomes	2.8	4.0	3.5	3.4	3.9	4.0	4.0	3.5
Public spending cuts too far	2.9	4.3	3.6	3.5	4.2	4.4	4.3	3.7
Environmental protection too far	2.9	2.5	2.3	3.1	1.6	1.5	2.4	2.6
Lib-Authoritarian index (0-20)	15	13	12	16	10	8	12	14
Immigration should be higher	1.7	2.2	2.3	1.4	2.6	3	2.5	1.9
% UK should leave EU	55	27	18	93	15	11	28	42
Satisfied with British democracy	2.9	2.2	2.3	2.1	1.8	1.6	1.8	2.4
Voting for a small party is a waste	2.9	2.9	2.3	2.1	1.7	1.6	2.1	2.7
N	8549	8787	2405	3248	1306	113	2475	41837

Fig. 6.1 Socio-demographic and attitudinal profiles by 2015 party choice

even younger, more female and more well-educated than the GPEW's, although slightly less non-White British. However, given the very low number of observations of Green voters in Scotland, we must treat these findings with considerable caution. In England and Wales, Green voters were the least likely to own their home and be religious, but most likely to be a full-time student. Again, the profile of the Scottish Greens' voters in 2015 was even more disproportionately non-home owning, non-religious and in full-time education than the Greens in England and Wales. Finally, the GPEW's voters were disproportionately drawn from higher social classes in a similar vein to the Conservatives' and Liberal Democrats' voters, although their incomes were around the national average and they did gain more of their voters from the very lowest social classes than either of those parties. By contrast, the Scottish Greens' 2015 voters appeared to be disproportionately of a lower class with below-average incomes. We must take this surprising finding with extreme caution given that only 64 respondents who voted Scottish Green gave any response regarding social class. This finding is also in contrast with the profile of who votes Green in the Scottish Parliament's regional list elections.

In terms of political attitudes, the GPEW's voters consider themselves to be more left wing than any other English party's voters. However, on the actual policy questions of whether government should redistribute wages and whether public spending cuts (austerity) have gone too far, GPEW voters in 2015 were actually slightly less left wing than Labour voters, Scottish Greens and SNP voters. Unsurprisingly, the GPEW and Scottish Greens' voters had the most pro-environmental attitudes of any party. Furthermore, both Green parties had the most libertarian voters, as measured by a libertarian-authoritarian index variable comprising five attitudinal responses.[2] Both parties' voters also have the most pro-immigration attitudes–though even the GPEW's voters lean towards responding that immigration should be reduced rather than increased–and the most pro-European attitudes. Finally, both of the Green parties' voters were more dissatisfied with British politics than voters of any other party and were least likely to believe that voting for a small party is a waste of time.

Overall, we can see that Green voters in 2015 had a unique socio-demographic and attitudinal profile. They were disproportionately young, female, university educated, renting their home, non-religious and (in England and Wales, at least) from higher social classes. Politically, they *saw* themselves as extremely left wing, though on economic issues of redistribution and austerity had less left-wing views than Labour voters. They were also highly environmentalist, libertarian, pro-immigration (by the electorate's standards) and pro-EU, with similar, though less moderate, views to the remaining Liberal Democrats. Like UKIP and the SNP–only more so–both Green parties' voters were highly disenchanted with British democracy. These findings are largely in line with those of the existing literature. While they offer a fairly clear picture of *who* voted Green, we must still expain *why* those who voted Green did so.

Why Voters Chose the Greens

In Fig. 6.2, I present the results of three logistic regression analyses that test the effects of the above variables on voting Green in 2015. These models test only respondents who were in constituencies with Green Party candidates and are initially separated between socio-demographics and political attitudes in line with the 'funnel of causality' (Hofferbert 1974), with the former acting as more distal causes for party choice and the latter giving more proximal explanations. First, in the purely socio-demographic model, there is evidence that *all* of the socio-demographic variables, except ethnicity, had statistically significant effects on voting Green in the direction that we would expect based on the descriptive analysis. The only slight exception is that the effect of a slightly lower than average household income–between £15,000 and £30,000–has a positive effect on voting Green. In short, controlling for other socio-demographic variables, being younger, being female, non-religious, of a higher social class, though with a relatively low income, having or currently studying for a university degree, renting, and not living in Scotland all increased the voter's chance of choosing the Greens.

In the political attitudes model, there is evidence that voters chose the Greens because of their anti-austerity, environmentalist, libertarian and pro-EU attitudes and because they were dissatisfied with British democracy and were relatively comfortable voting for a small party. However, there is no evidence that having left-wing attitudes on the classic issue of redistribution of wealth increased one's chance of voting Green, nor that people voted Green because of their pro-immigration sentiment. I exclude left-right self-placement from the models because of its high multi-collinearity with each of the separate policy attitudes.

	Model 1: Socio Demographics	*Model 2: Political attitudes*	*Model 3: Combined Model*
Age	0.974***		0.981***
	(0.0032)		(0.0040)
Gender (male)	0.779**		0.644***
	(0.0694)		(0.0721)
Ethnicity (white)	1.009		
	(0.1495)		
University Degree	1.773***		1.065
	(0.1741)		(0.1362)
Homeowner	0.653***		0.886
	(0.0686)		(0.1210)
Student	1.615**		1.281
	(0.2709)		(0.2759)
No religion	2.121***		1.190
	(0.1961)		(0.1431)
Class (ref: missing)			
Higher professional/Managerial	1.659**		1.386
	(0.2772)		(0.2857)
Lower professional/Intermediate	1.280*		1.380*
	(0.1539)		(0.2186)
Small employer / Lower supervisory	1.0898		1.063
	(0.1939)		(0.2432)
Routine / Semi-routine	1.161		1.354
	(0.2031)		(0.2988)
Household Income (ref: refused to answer)			
£45,000+	1.005		1.182
	(0.1626)		(0.2343)
£30,000-£44,999	1.064		1.143
	(0.1450)		(0.1944)
£15,000-£29,999	1.382**		1.308
	(0.1650)		(0.1999)
£0-£14,999	1.166		1.108
	(0.01559)		(0.1844)
Scotland	0.636**		0.282***
	(0.1122)		(0.0558)
Govt should redistribute incomes		1.083	
		(0.0597)	
Public spending cuts too far		1.181**	1.285***
		(0.0756)	(0.0829)
Enviro protection gone too far		0.408***	0.410***
		(0.0312)	(0.3274)
Authoritarian-Libertarian index		0.943***	0.949***
		(0.1261)	(0.0138)
Immigration should be increased		1.095	
		(0.0558)	
UK should leave EU		0.680*	0.673*
		(0.1092)	(0.1104)
Satisfied with UK democracy		0.735***	0.695***
		(0.0467)	(0.0476)
Voting for a small party is a waste		0.486***	0.478***
		(0.0296)	(0.0313)
Constant	0.083***	1.962	5.354***
	(0.0179)	(0.8745)	(2.6157)
Pseudo R2	0.082	0.238	0.266
Observations	22467	16752	16200

*** p<0.001, ** p<0.01, * p<0.05 ; Odds Ratios Reported

Fig. 6.2 Determinants of voting Green in the 2015 UK General Election

In the final model, which combines those variables with statistically significant effects from the two separate models, there is far weaker evidence of socio-demographic effects when controlling for political attitudes. Only youth, being female and living outside of Scotland are shown to have a positive effect on voting Green, as well as being in a lower professional or intermediate social class. By contrast, the effects of the political attitudinal variables remain and are all either strengthened or remain the same. This full model still manages to explain just a quarter of variance in voting for the Greens, suggesting that there is still some way to go to fully understand the causes of voting Green.

In order to better compare the determinants of voting Green, the marginal effect of a one standard deviation increase of each statistically significant variable from the above combined model is shown in Fig. 6.3. The two most powerful explanations for Green voting were the belief that voting for a small party is not a wasted vote and environmentalism, both

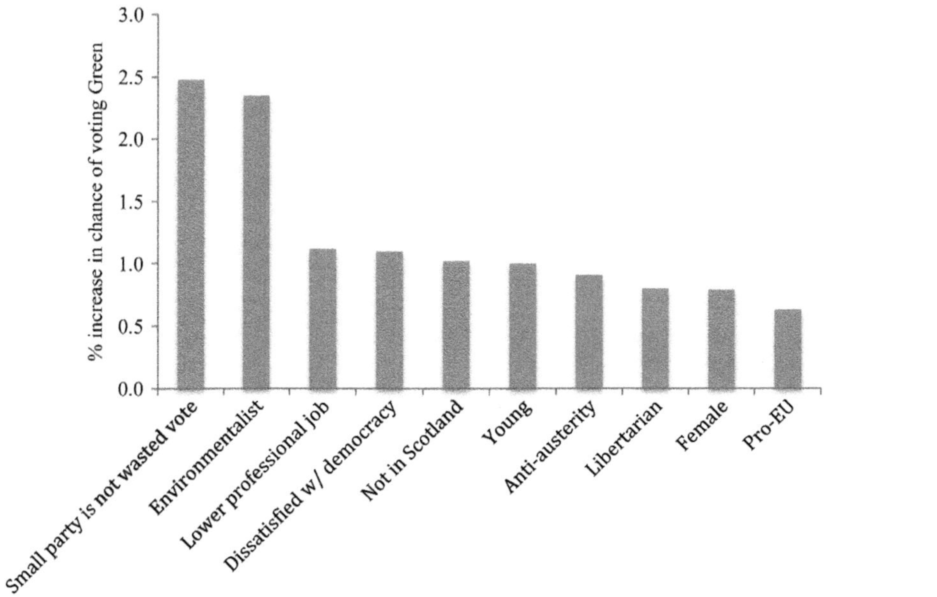

Fig. 6.3 Marginal effects of statistically significant predictors of voting Green

of which increased the chance of voting Green by around 2.5 per cent. Their maximum effects, when increasing each variable from its minimum to maximum response, were both an 8.5 per cent increase in likelihood of voting Green. The other determinants of voting Green had similar effects of between 0.5 per cent and 1.1 per cent, with higher class the most important socio-demographic variable and anti-austerity the strongest policy variable.

While these estimated effects give us a good idea of what caused voters to choose the Greens out of the electorate as a whole, we can further explain support for the Greens by separating these analyses by the political background of the respondent. I choose two backgrounds that provided a significant source of new Green voters in 2015 – first, 2010 Liberal Democrat voters (54 per cent of the Greens' 2015 voters) and, second, voters who had at some point between February 2014 and May 2015 planned on voting for, or did vote for, Labour in 2015 (29 per cent of the Greens' 2015 voters).

In Fig. 6.4, we can see that voters, of 2010 Liberal Democrats, being younger, female and *either* of a very high (higher professional or managerial) or very low (routine or semi-routine work) social class–though with a lower than average household income–had a positive effect on one's chance of voting Green. In policy terms, anti-austerity and strongly environmentalist views increased 2010 Liberal Democrats' chance of switching to the Greens–as well as being less satisfied with British democracy and more comfortable voting for a small party.

By contrast, the determinants of voting Green, of those intending to vote Labour in early 2014, were quite distinct. Youth, not owning a home, being a student and not living in Scotland all increased their chance of voting Green, when controlling for attitudinal variables. In contrast to the ex-Liberal Democrats, having a lower professional or intermediate job increased their chance of voting Green. Politically, those planning on voting Labour in early 2014 were more likely to switch to the Greens not because of anti-austerity or classically left-wing sentiment, but instead because of their environmentalist and libertarian outlooks. Again, we see evidence that dissatisfaction with UK democracy and willingness to vote for a small party positively affected their chance of voting Green.

	Model 1: 2010 Liberal Democrat voters – combined model	*Model 2: Early 2014 Labour vote intention – combined model*
Age	0.969***	0.987*
	(0.0056)	(0.0062)
Gender (male)		
Ethnicity (white)		
University Degree	1.1015	1.040
	(0.1760)	(0.2033)
Homeowner	0.915	0.673*
	(0.1613)	(0.1296)
Student		1.991*
		(0.6623)
No religion	1.257	1.022
	(0.2076)	(0.1814)
Class (ref: missing)		
Higher professional/Managerial	1.737*	1.708
	(0.4452)	(0.4818)
Lower professional/Intermediate	1.501*	1.703*
	(0.3077)	(0.4317)
Small employer / Lower supervisory	1.006	1.092
	(0.2897)	(0.3978)
Routine / Semi-routine	1.961*	1.217
	(0.5745)	(0.3993)
Household Income (ref: refused to answer)		
£45,000+	1.225	
	(0.3490)	
£30,000-£44,999	0.999	
	(0.2267)	
£15,000-£29,999	1.746**	
	(0.3574)	
£0-£14,999	1.039	
	(0.2481)	
Scotland	0.605	0.259***
	(0.1706)	(0.0883)
Govt should redistribute incomes		
Public spending cuts too far	1.431***	
	(0.1322)	
Enviro protection gone too far	0.442***	0.546***
	(0.0474)	(0.0701)
Authoritarian-Libertarian index		0.922***
		(0.0168)
Immigration should be increased		
UK should leave EU		
Satisfied with UK democracy	0.717***	0.7592**
	(0.0712)	(0.0806)
Voting for a small party is a waste	0.523***	0.504***
	(0.0467)	(0.0498)
Constant	2.295	4.304
	(1.5089)	(2.2370)
Pseudo R2	0.200	0.181
Observations	4491	7243

*** p<0.001, ** p<0.01, * p<0.05 ; Odds Ratios Reported

Fig. 6.4 Determinants of voting Green (of (1) 2010 Liberal Democrat voters and (2) those who had intended to vote Labour in early 2014)

Leader, Competence and Contact Effects

Party leader effects are excluded from the above regression analyses because of the endogeneity between party choice and leader affinity (Evans and Anderson 2005). Perception of party competence and party contact are excluded for similar reasons. Instead, I present fixed effects logistic panel models of the effects of these three variables on voting, or intention to vote, for the Green Party. The advantage of fixed effects panel data models is that they isolate the effects of variance *within* each respondent (i.e. over time) and thus inherently control for any unobserved, non-varying confounding effects within the individual, a common source of endogeneity. This does not entirely remove the potential for endogeneity–the dependent variable may still affect the independent variable–but it does remove an important and, intuitively, more likely source of bias. The primary disadvantage of these models is that they cannot test for the effects of non-varying variables and, as such, those individuals that do not vary in the dependent or independent variables are dropped from the model, resulting in relatively low numbers of observations.

I compare the effects of leader affinity, perception of party competence and party contact of each of the Conservatives, Labour, the Liberal Democrats, UKIP and the Greens. Leader affinity ('How much do you like or dislike the following party leaders?') is measured on a 0–10 scale for each of the five leaders. Party competence is also measured on a 0–10 scale that asks how well each party would handle the respondent's 'most important issue'. Finally, party contact is a binary variable that asks whether the respondent has been contacted by each party over the last four weeks (or the four weeks prior to the election). The effects of these variables are only included for the Greens in the final three waves of the six waves of the 2014–2017 BES. I test each party's three variables in separate models–totalling 15 models–and only include observations from the final three waves, to ensure fairer comparability with the Greens. To control for contemporaneous political context, I also include a categorical variable of each wave (Fig. 6.5).

We see evidence of a positive effect of leader affinity on likelihood of voting for each of the parties. However, this effect was weakest for the Green Party, suggesting that their vote was *relatively* unaffected by how much voters liked Natalie Bennett as an individual. By contrast, no party's image of competence affected vote intention more than the Green Party's–Green support was especially subject to how well the voter thought the

	Greens			Conservatives		
Leader affinity	1.24***			1.34***		
Party competence		1.29***			1.19***	
Party contact			1.21			0.88
Wave (ref: 4)						
5	0.64***	0.50***	0.57**	1.16***	1.28**	1.10
6	0.69***	0.43***	0.62***	1.78***	1.71***	1.76***
Observations	2630	583	833	8707	1758	1713
Individuals	960	210	373	3075	631	765

	Labour			Liberal Democrats		
Leader affinity	1.31***			1.32***		
Party competence		1.17***			1.16***	
Party contact			1.22			1.03
Wave (ref: 4)						
5	1.03	1.07	1.07	1.83***	1.97***	2.23***
6	1.79***	1.67***	1.82***	3.27***	4.42***	3.22***
Observations	8789	1775	1916	5269	1002	1356
Individuals	3114	641	846	1850	359	595

	UKIP			
Leader affinity	1.37***			
Party competence		1.20***		
Party contact			1.13	*** p<0.001
Wave (ref: 4)				** p<0.01
5	0.55***	0.46***	0.48***	* p<0.05
6	0.46***	0.41***	0.40***	Odds Ratios Reported
Observations	5926	1245	1014	
Individuals	2090	452	452	

Fig. 6.5 Fixed effects logistic panel models of leader affinity, party competence and party contact effects

party would deal with their 'most important issue'. Finally, the effect of receiving contact from the Greens on voting Green was higher than the equivalent effect of any other party–besides Labour. However, these contact effects were not statistically significant.

Overall, the Green Party in 2015 attracted a segment of the British electorate with a clear profile. In socio-demographic terms, these voters were young, female, university educated, house renters, non-religious and of a similar social class to Conservative and Liberal Democrat voters, though with lower incomes. Politically, Green voters could be described as leftist–though no more than Labour voters–libertarian and internationalist, as well as being highly disenchanted with modern British politics. These voters were drawn to the Greens most keenly because they were willing to vote for a smaller party and because of their environmentalism–though their socio-demographic profiles and their anti-austerity, anti-establishment and libertarian attitudes also contributed to their decision. Whereas classically leftist attitudes on redistribution played no part in attracting voters to the Greens, the highly salient and contemporary issue of austerity, and Green voters' opposition to it, was a strong motivation for voting Green. The motivations for Green support varied between 2010 Liberal Democrats and those who had planned on voting Labour in early 2014. Ex-Lib Dems were more likely to vote Green if they had either very high or very low social class and lower than average incomes and were opposed to austerity, whereas the latter Labour sympathisers were more likely to vote Green if they had intermediate jobs and more libertarian outlooks, as well as being home renters. It would seem that defectors to the Greens were simply less willing to tolerate Miliband's ambiguous and accommodating stance to the right on the issues of austerity and immigration than Labour voters, despite having practically identical views to Labour voters. Finally, the Greens' vote was particularly subject to perceptions of competence in the final months before the election, while affinity towards Natalie Bennett played a weaker role, particularly by the standards of leader effects from other parties.

Notes

1. It seems that the reason for the low proportion of White British citizens voting Green is not because of ethnic diversity but at least partially because of the Greens' ability to attract British citizens born in EU member states – ten per cent of whom voted Green in 2015, compared to just 3.5 per cent of those born in Commonwealth countries.
2. The responses are to the statements: 'People who break the law should be given stricter sentences', 'Censorship of films and magazines is necessary to uphold moral standards', 'Schools should teach children to obey authority', 'For some crimes, the death penalty is the most appropriate sentence' and 'Young people today don't have enough respect for traditional British values'.

Bibliography

Bennulf, M. and Holmberg, S. (1990), 'The Green Breakthrough in Sweden' in *Scandinavian Political Studies*, 13 (2), 165–84

Birch, S. (2009), 'Real Progress: Prospect for Green Party Support in Britain' in *Parliamentary Affairs*, 62 (1), 53–71

Clarke, H., Kellner, P., Stewart, M. C., Twyman, J. and Whiteley, P. (2016), *Austerity and Political Choice in Britain*, Basingstoke: Palgrave

Dennison, J. (2015) 'The Other Insurgency? The Greens and the Election' in *Parliamentary Affairs*, 68 (suppl 1), 188–205

Dolezal, M. (2010), 'Exploring the Stabilization of a Political Force: The Social and Attitudinal Basis of Green Parties in the Age of Globalization' in *West European Politics*, 33, 534–552

Evans, G. and Anderson, T. (2005), 'The Impact of Party Leaders: How Blair Lost Labour Voters' in *Parliamentary Affairs*, 58 (4), 818–836

Hofferbert, R. (1974), *The Study of Public Policy*, Indianapolis: Bobbs-Merrill

Inglehart, R. (1977), The Silent Revolution. Changing Values and Political Styles among Western Publics, Princeton: Princeton University Press.

Kitschelt, H. (1990) 'New Social Movements and the Decline of Party Organization' in R. Dalton & M. Kuechler (eds), Challenging the Political Order, Cambridge: Polity Press: 179–208

Kreuzer, M. (1990), 'New Politics: Just Post-Materialist? The Case of the Austrian and Swiss Greens' in West European Politics, 13, 12–30

Kriesi, H., Grande, E., Lachat, R., Dolezal, M., Bornschier, S. and Frey, T. (2008), *West European Politics in the Age of Globalisation*, Cambridge: Cambridge University Press

Müller-Rommel, F. (1985), 'The Greens in Western Europe: Similar but Different' in *International Political Science Review*, 6, 483–99

Müller-Rommel, F. (1990) 'New Political Movements and "New Politics" Parties in Western Europe' in R. Dalton & M. Kuechler (eds), Challenging the Political Order, Cambridge: Polity Press: 209–301

Poguntke, T. (1989), *Alternative Politics: The German Green Party*, Edinburgh: Edinburgh University Press

Rüdig, W. (1990) 'Explaining Green Party Development' in Strathclyde Papers on Government and Politics, No. 71

CHAPTER 7

Explaining Constituency-Level Green Success

Abstract In this chapter, I move from an individual-level explanation of variation in voting for the Green Party to an aggregate-level one. Building upon previous analyses, I consider what socio-demographic and political aspects affected the Green Party of England and Wales' constituency vote share. I also incorporate data on the Green Party's constituency-level campaigning strategy in order to produce a model that predicts Green Party constituency vote share in 2015. I use this model to compare each constituency's predicted vote share and its actual 2015 vote share, producing a table of the 30 'best' and 'worst' constituency electoral performances. Finally, I consider the commonalities between those constituencies that performed unexpectedly well and badly, respectively, finding that the Greens' own activities best explain this residual.

Keywords Green Party • Constituency effects • Party choice • General election • Campaigning

Determinants of Green Party Constituency Vote Share

Although we now have a clearer understanding of what caused some individuals to vote Green in the 2015 general election, this cannot reliably explain the considerable variation in the Greens' vote share by constituency

J. Dennison, *The Greens in British Politics*,
DOI 10.1007/978-3-319-42673-0_7

(known as the 'ecological fallacy', see Kramer 1983). The party's mean vote share was 4.2 per cent in seats in which it stood a candidate, making the standard deviation of 2.8 fairly high. Overall, the vote share ranged from 0.9 to 41.8, with the upper quartile starting at 4.7. Such variation suggests that a considerable portion of the explanation for the quadrupling of the Greens' vote share lies in constituency-level, rather than individual-level, factors. This chapter will therefore attempt to explain the considerable variation in the Greens' constituency vote share in 2015.

Two recent works have tested constituency-level Green Party results. Birch (2009) found evidence that the party's 2005 General Election constituency results could be explained by the positive effects of the area's proportion of students, population density, proportion of residents who respond as having no religion and the size of the winning party's constituency majority. Regarding the 2015 General Election, Clarke et al. (2016: 140) found that the Greens' constituency vote share could be explained more by urban density than could the vote share of any other party and that a constituency's proportion of Muslims had a negative effect on the Green vote, whereas the constituency's ethnic minority population had a positive effect.

In addition to findings from the literature, socio-demographic variables from the previous chapter can be tested at the constituency level. These comprise the constituency's average age, home ownership rate and proportion of residents with a university education. In order to capture some of the economic profile of the constituency, I include the local unemployment rate. To distinguish between ethnic diversity and national diversity, I include separate variables to capture the constituency's non-white population and its non-British citizen population. Beyond socio-demographics, earlier evidence that a majority of 2015 Greens voted for the Liberal Democrats in 2010 suggests that including the Liberal Democrats' 2010 performance may explain Green voting in 2015. Two other key political variables are the Greens' 2010 performance and a dummy variable to capture the different party system in Wales. Furthermore, I add an ordinal variable to capture the Greens' five-tier constituency targeting strategy, which redirected funds towards the selected 16 seats according to their placement within those tiers.[1]

As with individual-level determinants of Green voting, I initially separate socio-demographic and political determinants, in line with the funnel of causality model (Hofferbert 1974). Furthermore, given the highly asymmetrical positive skew of the distribution of Green Party vote percentages in 2015, I take the log of the Greens' vote as the dependent variable. I do the same for the independent variables measuring the Greens' 2010 constituency performances, as well as the 2015 constituency majority[2] and 2010 Liberal Democrat vote share. Only English and Welsh constituencies in which the Green Party of England and Wales (GPEW) stood a candidate are tested and the speaker's seat is not included in the latter two models. The results of these three analyses are shown in Fig. 7.1.

The socio-demographic model is able to explain over a half of the variance in 2015 Green Party vote share. Interestingly, this model neither finds evidence of an effect of the constituency's population density nor of its Muslim population, contrary to the findings of Clarke et al. (2016). However, as Clarke et al. find, there is evidence that greater ethnic diversity has a positive effect, though, conversely, a larger non-British population decreases the Greens' vote share. The party can thus expect to do better in ethnically heterogeneous though nationally homogenous areas, when other factors are controlled for. In common with the findings of Birch (2009), a larger student population and a less religious constituency electorate both increase the Green Party's vote share. In line with the individual-level findings, more home renting and a better educated, less economically deprived electorate are likely to result in better Green performances. Most surprisingly, a higher proportion of the electorate who are under 30 years old has the effect of *lowering* the Greens' vote share, when controlling for the effects of other variables such as having or currently receiving university education and home renting.

The political model has an even higher predictive power and offers evidence that all of the independent variables have the predicted effects on Green Party constituency vote share. A less marginal political context has a positive effect on the GPEW's performance as voters are both less incentivised to vote tactically and are likely to receive less campaign contact from mainstream parties than in marginal seats. A higher Liberal Democrat vote share in 2010 had a positive effect on the Greens' performance in 2015, as a higher number of disenchanted ex-Liberal Democrats– often with similar profiles to those of the Green voters–searched for a new party. Unsurprisingly, the model offers evidence that the Greens' 2010 performance had a positive effect on the party's 2015 performance; however, its relatively small effect is testament to the size of the party's growth since then. The GPEW's performances in Wales were negatively affected by some distinct effect aside from those being controlled for–I would theorise that this would be the greater competition that the party faces from

Dependent variable: log(GPEW vote share)	*Model 1: Socio Demographics*	*Model 2: Political profile*	*Model 3: Combined Model*
% Student	0.0487*** (0.0095)		0.0265*** (0.0069)
Population density (urbanity)	0.0020 (0.0012)		
% No religion	0.0155*** (0.0036)		0.0125*** (0.0024)
% Muslim	0.0011 (0.0037)		
% Ethnic Minority	0.0152*** (0.0046)		0.0088** (0.0029)
% non-British	-0.0298*** (0.0056)		-0.0187*** (0.0042)
% Under 30	-0.0592*** (0.0117)		-0.0304*** (0.0082)
% Home Owner	-0.0398*** (0.0033)		-0.0264*** (0.0027)
% University Degree	0.0106*** (0.0226)		0.0075*** (0.0023)
% Unemployed	-0.2178*** (0.0227)		-0.1182*** (0.0185)
Log % Majority in 2015		0.0987*** (0.0160)	0.1018*** (0.0135)
Log % Liberal Democrats in 2010		0.4474*** (0.0357)	0.2383*** (0.0373)
Log % Greens in 2010		0.3617*** (0.0285)	0.1954*** (0.0251)
Wales		-0.1283* (0.0503)	-0.2591*** (0.0445)
Target (ref: not)			
Tier 5 – 'Supported'		0.3314** (0.1074)	0.1513 (0.1097)
Tier 4 – 'Development'		0.5479*** (0.1333)	0.2664*** (0.0550)
Tier 3 – 'Advanced'		0.3577 (0.1986)	0.1104 (0.0641)
Tier 2 – 'Target'		0.8598* (0.3349)	0.5339* (0.2451)
Tier 1 – 'Held'		1.5850*** (0.0901)	1.2828*** (0.0835)
Constant	4.9005*** (0.3868)	-0.5475*** (0.1067)	2.3309*** (0.3564)
R^2	0.5515	0.5976	0.7340
Observations	537	536	536

*** p<0.001, ** p<0.01, * p<0.05 ; Odds Ratios and Robust Standard Errors reported

Fig. 7.1 Determinants of GPEW constituency vote share

the similarly left-libertarian Plaid Cymru there. There is also strong evidence in the political model that the GPEW's targeting strategy positively affected the party's performance in the selected constituencies.

The combined model of all of the statistically significant socio-demographic and political variables is able to predict nearly three-quarters of variation in the GPEW's constituency vote share in 2015. The effect of a one standard deviation increase in each of these determinants is shown in Fig. 7.2. In descending order, the most powerful determinants of GPEW support were a lower proportion of home owners, fewer non-British residents, fewer unemployed residents and fewer under 30s, followed by a higher proportion of students and non-white residents.

Using the combined model we are able to predict the vote share of the Green Party in each constituency with some accuracy (Goodwin and Milazzo 2015 performed a similar exercise for UKIP vote share). By then comparing the constituency party's actual and predicted vote share, we can consider which were the 'best' and 'worst' Green Party performance, when controlling for the local socio-demographic and political factors. This allows for a more qualitative analysis of the commonalities between these two sets of 15 constituencies, respectively, which should give us further insight into the determinants of constituency GPEW vote

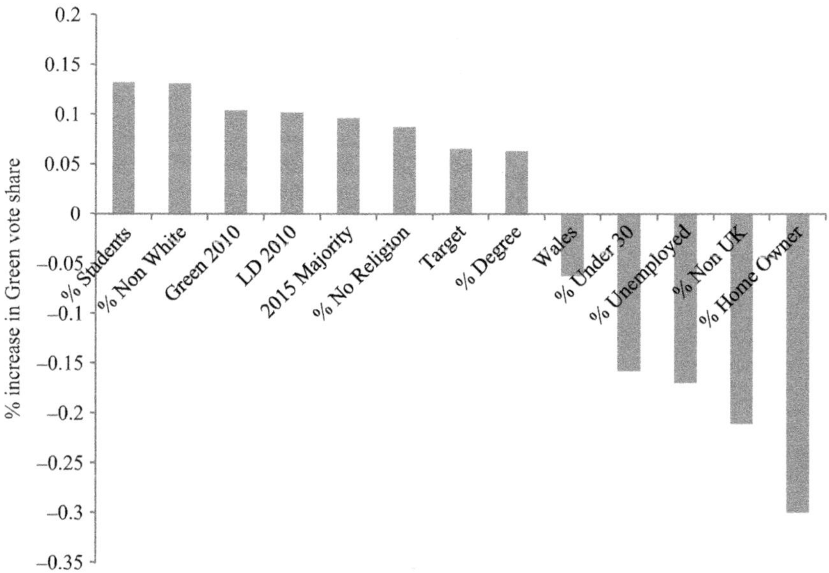

Fig. 7.2 Marginal effects of determinants of 2015 GPEW vote share

Rank	Constituency Name	Actual	Predicted	Difference
1	Isle of Wight	13.4	4.1	+9.3
2	Bristol West	26.8	19.3	+7.6
3	Bristol South	11.5	5.7	+5.8
4	Hackney North and Stoke Newington	14.6	8.9	+5.7
5	Tottenham	9.2	4.7	+4.5
6	Somerton and Frome	9.0	4.7	+4.3
7	Totnes	10.3	6.0	+4.3
8	Bristol East	8.3	4.3	+4.0
9	Lewisham, Deptford	12.5	9.1	+3.4
10	Central Devon	8.9	5.7	+3.3
11	Leyton and Wanstead	7.3	4.2	+3.1
12	Hereford and South Herefordshire	7.2	4.2	+3.1
13	Bournemouth East	7.3	4.4	+2.9
14	Nottingham East	9.9	7.0	+2.8
15	Bath	11.9	9.1	+2.8
...				
523	Hornsey and Wood Green	5.4	7.0	-1.6
524	The Cotswolds	4.6	6.2	-1.6
525	Maidstone and The Weald	2.8	4.4	-1.6
526	Westmorland and Lonsdale	3.7	5.3	-1.6
527	Watford	2.4	4.1	-1.7
528	St Albans	3.7	5.4	-1.7
529	Nottingham South	5.4	7.2	-1.8
530	Greenwich and Woolwich	6.4	8.4	-2.0
531	Chesterfield	3.0	5.0	-2.0
532	Oxford West and Abingdon	4.4	6.5	-2.2
533	Birmingham, Ladywood	4.2	6.4	-2.2
534	Welwyn Hatfield	3.5	5.9	-2.5
535	Sheffield, Hallam	3.2	5.9	-2.7
536	Bermondsey and Old Southwark	3.9	8.2	-4.3
537	Norwich South	13.9	19.4	-5.5

Fig. 7.3 The GPEW's fifteen 'best' and 'worst' performing constituencies

share. Fig. 7.3 presents the top fifteen 'over-performing' Green constituencies and the top fifteen 'under-performing' constituencies.

The discrepancies between the over-performing and under-performing constituencies fall into at least three clear categories. First, in geographical terms, the over-performing constituencies are all, with the one exception of Nottingham East, in the south of England. Indeed, three are in the city of Bristol, which itself only comprises four constituencies, and another four are elsewhere in the South West of England, meaning that nearly half of the fifteen over-performers are in just one region. Four of the remaining eight are in London,[3] with another two on the south coast. In contrast, five of the fifteen under-performing seats are outside of the south of England, with zero in the South West.

Why would the Greens do better in some regions than others, even when we have controlled for socio-demographic and political factors? Part of the reason appears to lie in the actions of the Liberal Democrats. Despite performing disproportionately well in the 2010 election in the south of England, the Liberal Democrats were left with only two MPs south of the Midlands in 2015. Indeed, the average Liberal Democrat collapse in the Greens' 15 over-performing constituencies was 23 per cent, compared to a national average of 15 per cent, which was also the average collapse in the most under-performing Green seats. However, this alone cannot satisfactorily explain the discrepancy between the two groups of Green seats – after all, the size of the Liberal Democrat collapse was partially a function of the Greens' performance itself.

However, the size of the Liberal collapse–and the resulting effect on the Greens–seems to be in part a function of the electoral priorities of Nick Clegg's party. In the Greens' most under-performing constituencies, they faced some of the most high-profile Liberal Democrat incumbent MPs in the country, including leader Nick Clegg in Sheffield Hallam, Simon Hughes in Bermondsey and Old Southwark, Tim Farron in Westmorland and Lonsdale and, of lesser prominence, local mayor Dorothy Thornhill in Watford and Lynne Featherstone in Hornsey and Wood Green. By contrast, in the GPEW's over-performing constituencies, the only prominent Liberal Democrat was Stephen Williams in Bristol West. This finding is supported by Gill Coombes, Green candidate for Totnes, who stated that the Liberal Democrat incumbent's "vote really did collapse completely and he just didn't even bother with the campaign." This can only explain the variance in Green success in a handful of the under-performing seats, however.

A far more consistent dissimilarity between the top and bottom performing constituencies was the actions of the constituency Green Party itself. In the over-performing seats, the party's candidates were in every case highly visible in local media. In the Isle of Wight, the GPEW were engaged in public events, social media, traditional advertising, including 'crowdfunding' a billboard, and numerous hustings. After one hustings, Green candidate Vix Lothian was voted as the best performing candidate, a feat reported in the local press.[4] In the Isle of Wight, the party also explicitly rejected the 'target-to-win' strategy, whereby campaigning would have been focussed on certain local election wards in which the Greens may have won a seat.

The advantage of participation in hustings was also pronounced in constituencies such as Bournemouth East, in which the debate was dominated by the issues of wind turbines, zero hours contracts and local spending cuts, and in constituencies such as Nottingham South, with particularly centrist Labour candidates. [5] In Tottenham, the local newspaper praised the GPEW candidate for having "every fact at her fingertips and a capacity for expressing her party's policies with sharp clarity."[6] Similarly, *The Guardian* described the Greens' candidate in Hackney North and Stoke Newington, Heather Finlay, as "articulate" with an "energetic local campaign."[7] In Leyton and Wanstead and Lewisham Deptford, both in east London, GPEW candidates won support at hustings for their promise to cap rents, as well as on the issues of health and Trident nuclear submarines.[8] In rural Conservative safe seats, such as Hereford and South Herefordshire, the party won support on the issue of fracking and other environmental and rural issues.[9] In Bath, the GPEW attempted to increase the profile of their parliamentary and local candidates with a series of publicised 'open house events', while the candidate in Bristol South increased his visibility by attending protest marches over rent increases.[10] In short, the Green Party's activities in their over-performing constituencies were highly visible and highly active, while their candidates were articulate and their policies were particularly relevant locally.

In the GPEW's most under-performing constituencies, such as Greenwich and Woolwich, Chesterfield, Birmingham Ladywood, Welwyn Hatfield and Bermondsey and Old Southwark, the party had little media visibility. In both the Cotswolds and Nottingham South, the Green candidate was the only party candidate to fail to attend local hustings, despite being invited.[11] In Nottingham South and Oxford West and Abingdon, the Greens suffered as Labour and the Liberal Democrats, respectively, were able to attract the student vote.[12] In Hornsey and Wood Green, Watford and Sheffield Hallam the Green vote shares were all possibly harmed by a *Guardian* article that listed them as three of the 16 constituencies where voters should avoid voting Green because of the tactical implications for Labour's hopes of forming a government.[13] Finally, a relatively low-profile campaign undermined the Green campaign in Norwich South, along with a candidate that led one *New Statesman* article to conclude that "the Greens probably didn't choose their candidate wisely."[14]

Overall, the Greens primarily lost out in these constituencies because of ineffective local parties and candidates.

Variation in the Green Party's 2015 constituency results can in part be explained by both previous findings from the literature and what we know about individual Green voters. A constituency with more renters, more students, a lower unemployment rate and more non-religious voters was likely to have a higher Green vote share. More surprising was that, with these factors controlled for, the effect of more voters under thirty years old and more non-British citizens was to reduce the Greens' local popularity. The political predictors for Green constituency success were perhaps more predicable–a less marginal seat, not facing the competition of left-libertarian nationalists, higher past Liberal Democrat support and past Green Party support–though the effect of the latter was fairly weak. Along with the Greens' targeting strategy, these factors were able to predict around three-quarters of variation in the party's constituency results.

By considering those constituencies for which the model had the weakest predictive power, we can draw out further nuance. The Greens clearly did better in the south of England than elsewhere and particularly in those areas most abandoned, electorally, by the Liberal Democrats. However, these factors seem to be overshadowed by the high variation in the GPEW's campaigning capability. In those areas in which the party had local marketing strategies, articulate candidates and took part fully in the constituency campaign process, such as in candidate debates, the party performed better than constituency socio-demographics and political history would predict. As with the national party, the Greens' constituency campaigns were not unanimously able to make the transition into a comprehensive electoral force. The rise in prominence of the national party saw a near-universal rise in the party's popularity–just two seats saw a decrease in vote share. However, only in those seats with a highly specific combination of socio-demographic and political factors, as well as an ambitious local party, were the Greens capable of making a more impressive impact. Ultimately, 15 per cent of the GPEW's total votes came from just four per cent of the constituencies in which they stood candidates.

Notes

1. (Tier 1) Held Seat: Brighton Pavilion; (2) Target Constituencies: Norwich South, Bristol West; (3) Advanced Constituencies: Solihull, Sheffield Central, Liverpool Riverside, Oxford East, St Ives; (4) Development

Constituencies: Reading East, Holborn and St Pancras, York Central; (5) Supported Constituencies: Lincoln City, Harrogate and Knaresborough, Chichester, Streatham, Greenwich and Woolwich.

2. Strictly, including the 2015 majority breaks the temporal ordering criteria of causality. However, given the stark changes to the party system since 2010, it is likely to better capture the voters' sense of constituency marginality *prior* to voting than, for example, the 2010 constituency majority.
3. All of which are east of Charing Cross, often used as the 'centre' of London.
4. Isle of Wight County Press (2015), '#iwvote: Green Party's Vix Lowthion tops Hustings poll', accessed at http://www.iwcp.co.uk/news/general-election-2015/iwvote-green-partys-vix-lowthion-tops-hustings-poll-80807.aspx on 22/4/2016.
5. Kuusio, E (2015), 'Bournemouth East hustings covers a wide range of issues', accessed at http://www.yourelection15.co.uk/news/04/16/bournemouth-east-hustings-covers-wide-range-issues/ on 22/4/2016.
6. Collins, S. (2015), 'Election 2015: Candidates clash at Tottenham hustings', accessed at http://www.tottenhamjournal.co.uk/seasonal/election/election_2015_candidates_clash_at_tottenham_hustings_1_4036281 on 22/4/2016.
7. Hill, D. (2015), 'Diane Abbott: Defending Hackney North with half an eye on City Hall', accessed at http://www.theguardian.com/uk-news/davehillblog/2015/apr/28/diane-abbott-defending-hackney-north-with-half-an-eye-on-city-hall on 22/04/2016.
8. Wyatt, B. (2015), 'Gallery: Health, housing and Trident debated at Wanstead husitngs', accessed at http://www.ilfordrecorder.co.uk/seasonal/election/gallery_health_housing_and_trident_debated_at_wanstead_hustings_1_4048921 on 22/04/2016.
9. WMNPBowern (2015), 'Time to show badgers dying from bovine TB on TV's Countryfile, say UKIP' accessed at http://www.westernmorningnews.co.uk/Time-badgers-dying-bovine-TB-Countryfile-says/story-26428738-detail/story.html on 22/04/2016.
10. Bath Chronicle (2015), 'Chance for people to meet Green Party candidates this weekend', accessed at http://www.bathchronicle.co.uk/Chance-people-meet-Green-Party-candidates-weekend/story-26336537-detail/story.html on 22/04/2016; Bristol Post (2015), 'Renters to demonstrate at CJ Hole Southvile branch after "cynical attempt to exploit tenants"', accessed at http://www.bristolpost.co.uk/Renters-demonstrate-CJ-Hole-Southville-branch/story-26317328-detail/story.html on 22/04/2016.
11. BBC News (2015), 'Cotswolds house-building process "outrageous" says election candidate', accessed at http://www.bbc.com/news/election-

2015-england-32348579 on 22/04/2016; Ireland, B. (2015), 'Election 2015: NHS dominates open-air Nottingham hustings debate', accessed at http://www.nottinghampost.com/Election-2015-NHS-dominates-open-air-Nottingham/story-26389213-detail/story.html on 22/04/2016.

12. Spring, M. (2015), 'Oxford students back Labour ahead of election', accessed at http://www.cherwell.org/2015/05/01/oxford-students-back-labour-ahead-of-election/ on 22/04/2016.
13. Monbiot, G. (2015), 'Just when hope and courage are called for, Labour promises bean-counting', accessed at http://www.theguardian.com/commentisfree/2015/apr/14/labour-bean-counting-hope-courage-deficit-voters on 22/04/2016.
14. Razavi, L. (2015), 'Why I'm voting Green', accessed at http://www.newstatesman.com/politics/2015/05/why-im-voting-green on 22/04/2016.

Bibliography

Birch, S. (2009), 'Real Progress: Prospect for Green Party Support in Britain' in *Parliamentary Affairs*, 62 (1), 53–71

Clarke, H., Kellner, P., Stewart, M. C., Twyman, J. and Whiteley, P. (2016), *Austerity and Political Choice in Britain*, Basingstoke: Palgrave

Goodwin, M. and Milazzo, C. (2015), *UKIP: Inside the Campaign to Redraw the Map of British Politics*, Oxford: Oxford University Press

Hofferbert, R. (1974), *The Study of Public Policy*, Indianapolis: Bobbs-Merrill

Kramer, G. H. (1983), 'The Ecological Fallacy Revisited: Aggregate- versus Individual-level Findings on Economic and Elections, and Sociotropic Voting' in *American Political Science Review*, 77(1), 92–11

CHAPTER 8

Conclusion: Protest, Anti-Austerity and the Divided Left

Abstract In the conclusion to *The Greens in British Politics*, I argue that central to the rise of the Greens was the issue of austerity, over which the Left in Britain and elsewhere has divided, and protest over the economic consensus of the past forty years. The Greens' new members and voters were an ideological coherent group who abandoned, first, the governing Liberal Democrats and, second, the ambiguous Labour Party. In both cases, the controversy over fiscal austerity was key whereas attitudes to issues like immigration were secondary. As such, if the newly popular Greens can be understood as a 'UKIP of the left', it is more in terms of protest than pro-immigration sentiment. Furthermore, I show how the growth and setbacks of the Green Party of England and Wales reflects the party's, at times difficult, transformation from a minor party into an accepted member of Britain's party system. I also show that the price of the party's transformation was a movement away from internal democracy. Looking forward, I speculate on the possible effect of Labour's new, leftist leader Jeremy Corbyn and place the rise of the Greens in comparative perspective.

Keywords Green Party • Anti-austerity • Protest • Jeremy Corbyn • Party system transformation • Scottish Greens

In the approach to the 2015 general election, the Green Party of England and Wales (GPEW) made a rapid transition from a minor party into a fully established member of the party system able to appeal to a clear section of

J. Dennison, *The Greens in British Politics*,
DOI 10.1007/978-3-319-42673-0_8

the electorate. Socially, Green voters in 2015 tended to be young, female, university educated, non-religious and in professional occupations, though with relatively low incomes. Politically, they were no more left-wing than Labour voters, particularly with regard to the classic left-wing concern of redistribution of incomes. Instead, environmentalism, libertarianism, opposition to austerity and a deep dissatisfaction with British democracy motivated this group, who were also far more likely to see voting in expressive terms than as an instrument to elect a government.

Largely thanks to the Green Surge, the GPEW enjoyed unprecedented exposure and resources, as membership fees and donations poured into the party from ideologically sympathetic members of the public. Greater resources allowed the party to stand candidates in the vast majority of constituencies across England and Wales and also deepened the potential for internal organisational change, as the party's administration transformed from the voluntary and disorganised structure of a minor party into having the full-time staff of an established party. Equipped with the salient message of anti-austerity, the GPEW, as the Liberal Democrats and UKIP had previously done, framed themselves *less* in the purely ideological terms of a minor party and increasingly as the alternative or 'real' opposition to the two parties of government. Owing to their democratic structure, as well as the rapidity of their rise in prominence, the party was unable to escape the cumulative policy commitments that it had amassed over the preceding forty years, which were similar to the ideological statements of a minor party and were used by the media consistently when scrutinising the party. However, the party did increasingly emphasise a small number of popular policies that had been ignored by the two parties of government—renationalising rail, a 'living wage' and a nationalised health service, in a similar fashion to the approaches of the Liberal Democrats and UKIP on other 'overlooked' issues.

At the moment that the Greens were admitted into the party system, the media's approach to the party rapidly switched from occasional event-driven interest to more thorough scrutiny. The party was plainly unprepared to deal with this change. Its leader, Natalie Bennett, who had been so successful in internal party politics, increasing the GPEW's visibility and at the more difficult job of increasing its relevance, was unable to maintain the credibility of her party at the first time of asking. Indeed, I find that the Greens' vote share was more subject to perceptions of competence than that of any other party in 2015. The GPEW, which was internally left shell-shocked by the harsh realities of electoral competition, immediately took on a risk-averse campaigning strategy and, so, fell back into their comfort zone of appeals to principle and protest rather than campaigning on key policies, personality or, even, tactical voting. As such, the Greens were unable to increase their seats or in the House of Commons. As Tom Beckett, GPEW Director for Fundraising and Operations, concludes, "We had no foundation before. We set the foundation; the Green Party has finally got a foundation of national support … If we'd been more pragmatic we could have gone even further. But that's political parties for you." For now, the GPEW have a somewhat secure standing, alongside the Liberal Democrats and UKIP, in the second tier of Britain's newly refigured party system.

How important was the government's fiscal austerity programme in explaining the rise of the Greens? I argue that austerity was a consistent factor in, first, the Liberal Democrat's loss of left-wing voters, the ambiguous message put forward by Labour, the increased relevance of the GPEW at the national level—particularly after the European elections—and in the decision of individuals to vote Green at the 2015 election. Had the government or official opposition explicitly framed their response to the economic crisis in terms of a 'fiscal stimulus', rather than austerity, the appeal of the Greens, their relevance and their media coverage would all have been fundamentally weaker. In particular, those who joined the GPEW either after the 2010 general election or during the Green Surge were opposed to public spending cuts in the strongest terms—more so than both the general public and, to a lesser extent, the Greens' pre-existing members. At the general election, anti-austerity sentiment had the largest positive effect on one's chance of voting Green of any policy position, besides environmentalism. By contrast, one's attitude to government redistribution of wealth, one of the traditional issues of left-right conflict, had no effect on one's chance of voting for the Greens in 2015. The positive effect of opposing austerity on voting Green is strengthened when we only consider those who voted for the Liberal Democrats in 2010, which was the source of half of the Greens' 2015 voters. The Liberal Democrats lost over half a million voters to the Greens by framing their sole mission in government as fiscal deficit reduction, primarily via spending cuts alongside the Conservatives. The Greens, however, failed to move beyond the essentially negative message of anti-austerity and towards campaigning on a positive policy offer of a fiscal stimulus. As such, opposition to austerity made the GPEW a strong protest choice but a weak policy choice.

The interaction between the Green Party and Labour during the 2015 election was less clear-cut than the unidirectional flow of voters away from the Liberal Democrats. The Greens won more voters from Labour than from any other party in the year and a half prior to the election but they also lost more voters to Labour than to any other party. For the Greens, this was a net gain—the former were double the latter. As former Secretary of State for Energy and Climate Change, 'Red Ed' Miliband should have been well placed to take the Greens' environmentalist, left-wing voters. I argue that he and his party were caught in a conundrum whereby any attempts to move Labour beyond the centrist 'New Labour' years necessitated a lurch to the left, thus playing into the argument of the Conservatives that Labour were fiscally reckless. In response, Labour proposed a long list of piecemeal left-wing policies but acquiesced to the need for austerity, as evidenced both in their rhetoric and in their rightward drift on tax and spending policies. Disenchanted Liberal Democrats had largely planned to vote for Labour. However, the Green Surge opened up the possibility of a new left-libertarian 'protest party'. Indeed, the Greens' new members around the time of the Green Surge saw Labour as a *right of centre* party, and the Greens as the only significant left-wing force left in England. In actual policy terms, Green voters in 2015 were practically identical on the issues of austerity and redistribution of wealth to Labour voters yet they thought of themselves as significantly more left wing. Green voters were also far more likely than Labour voters to be dissatisfied with British politics and be willing to vote for a small party. I show that Green voters who defected from Labour did so far less on policy grounds than those who defected from the Liberal Democrats, who had switched over the coalition government's austerity programme. Instead, socio-demographics played a stronger role, with youth, home renting, being a student and having intermediate job position all increasing the chance of defecting to the Greens from Labour. Where policy did matter, it was in terms of environmentalism and libertarianism, as well as protest, and not in terms of economics, about which Green and Labour voters were largely in agreement. Put simply, younger voters were less willing to tolerate the ambiguous and accommodating stance of Ed Miliband's Labour Party towards austerity and anti-immigration rhetoric than older voters were and so were more likely to vote for the Greens, even if the two groups held similar beliefs on classic left-right issues.

Were the Greens the 'UKIP of the left'? If, by this phrase, we mean the anti-pole to the radical right on an emerging European 'integration-demarcation' cultural divide, the evidence is mixed. The outrage, in some quarters of the electorate, over the GPEW's exclusion from the leaders' debates stemmed, at least in part, from the fact that the anti-immigration UKIP had been included. This was interpreted by some on the left as the final nail in the coffin of the pro-immigration, pro-multiculturalist consensus of the late 1990s and early 2000s. The individuals who were subsequently mobilised to join the GPEW did indeed have highly pro-immigration and pro-European views, in line with the party's pre-existing members. Also, there is evidence that pro-immigration, pro-European and anti-nationalist sentiments were factors in the choice of some pro-independence Scottish voters to join the Scottish Greens', following the Independence Referendum, rather than the Scottish National Party. However, the evidence from the general election is more ambiguous. Neither the voters of the GPEW nor of the Scottish Greens believed that immigration should be increased, even if their opposition to further immigration was far weaker than that of other parties—though it should be noted that their attitudes to European integration were very positive. This study found no evidence that pro-immigration sentiment was a factor in the decision to vote Green at the 2015 general election, though pro-Europeanism was a factor. It appears that the Greens' pro-immigration messaging was more useful in that it acted as a signal to voters that underscored the party's left-wing, cosmopolitan credentials and uncompromising attitude to the radical right.

However, if, by 'UKIP of the Left', we simply mean a left wing, protest party, then the data is unequivocal. The voters of UKIP and the GPEW were the most dissatisfied with British democracy of any parties in England. The Scottish Greens' voters were *even* more dissatisfied with British democracy than voters of the SNP. Moreover, the Greens occasionally incorporated populist language of a 'pure people' and 'corrupt elite', though still nowhere near to the extent that UKIP used this dichotomy. Interestingly, Green insiders were far more likely to describe themselves as the British equivalent to the Greek and Spanish leftist populists, Syriza and Podemos, than they ever were to compare themselves to other European Green parties, suggesting that some Greens would have been relatively happy to take on such a role in British politics. Unlike these parties, and UKIP, the GPEW was unable to pursue a charismatic electoral strategy that stressed the personality of its leader.

What does the rise of the Greens tell us about the role of the media in British politics? Following the passage of the Fixed Term Parliaments Act and the resulting lengthy coverage of the general election's 'horse race', journalists were incentivised to greet any growth in Green in support with far more enthusiasm and coverage than they had done before. During the Greens' 'discovery' phase, the media eagerly covered the party before the 'short campaign' had got underway. This, along with the Conservatives' desire to divide the left, played a significant role in the coverage that the controversy over the leaders' debates, and thus the Green Party, received. Once the Greens' inclusion in the debates and, implicitly, in the party system had become a fait accompli, the media, with impressive uniformity and rapidity, immediately turned to scrutinising the party, with devastating effect, before briskly moving on to 'more serious' matters.

After its rapid professionalisation and more gradual re-focus towards social justice, how far has the GPEW strayed from its green philosophical roots? Ideologically, the days of no-growth and population reduction were already long gone before 2015. However, environmentalism remained the biggest policy factor in determining whether one joined the Greens, rather than the SNP, after the independence referendum and whether one voted for the Greens at the 2015 general election. Green philosophical thought was never solely based on environmentalism, however, and there is evidence that the Greens' libertarian and anti-authority message attracted voters in 2015. The GPEW's biggest departure from their ideological roots came in the increased willingness of its leadership to circumvent internal democratic procedures on issues of policy and budgetary control in the high-pressure context of the year prior to the general election. Within the GPEW, resource distribution and decision-making power was increasingly centralised, both hierarchically and geographically, towards a small group of professional directors, the professional leadership and the party's single MP, as this group focused on vote and seat maximisation. Compared to other British parties, however, the Greens' remain highly internally democratic.

Did the Greens contribute to Britain's gradual transition from a two-party system to a multi-party system, or were they the result of that transition? Given that the decline of the two-party system, as measured by the percentage of voters opting for either the Conservatives or Labour, had been practically continuous since the 1950s, the latter seems far more likely. The most proximal cause for much of the two-party system's decline was the rise of the Liberal Democrats as an alternative third party from the 1970s onwards, particularly in constituencies in which one of the two parties of government made for an ineffective opposition. In 2015, the Liberal Democrats' vote collapsed as they retreated to the few seats that they maintained a realistic chance of defending. Aside from the GPEW's stronghold of Brighton and the particularly 'green' city of Bristol, the GPEW did best in Labour or Conservative safe-seats where a high proportion of highly educated, mid-income, non-religious, house-renters coalesced around the best placed party to appeal to left-libertarian voters. Even in these seats, the Greens were only able to move beyond a single-figure vote share when their local party was particularly well organised. Had the national GPEW not been as well organised as it was, the Greens' ability to attract disaffected Liberal Democrats and Labour voters would have been weaker and, given the dearth in other minor left-wing parties—with the possible exception of RESPECT—we can imagine that Britain's transition into a truly multi-party system would have been curtailed, though only slightly and, probably, temporarily.

Although Britain's political landscape has become gradually fragmented over the past fifty years, over the course of just one year, three events—the rise of the SNP, the Green Surge and Jeremy Corbyn's 2015 election as Labour leader—exposed the left's divide over the issue of austerity. To what extent were these three events part of a singular trend? Already, I argue that the issue of austerity was a more consistent and fundamental reason for the rise of the Greens than other salient issues, such as immigration. Scholars seeking to explain the SNP's landslide victory in Scotland in the 2015 general election note that "The SNP articulated an anti-austerity message throughout the campaign, as they had during the referendum ... Labour's uneasy balance in opposing Conservative austerity policies while avoiding resurrecting images of 'fiscal incontinence' was made more difficult by SNP demands to take sides in a progressive alliance"(Mitchell 2015: 95–95). Indeed, I show that in the aftermath to the independence referendum, SNP supporters were considerably more opposed to austerity than the electorate and that attitudes to austerity were unable to predict support for the Greens, rather than the SNP, amongst pro-independence Scots, suggesting that both groups were similarly opposed to the government's fiscal programme. In the Labour leadership election, one year later, it seems probable that anti-austerity sentiment was an important factor in the surprise election of Jeremy Corbyn by "Labour supporters who have concluded that the 'austerity light' policies espoused by Ed Miliband are contrary to the historic ideals of the party" (Clarke et al. 2016: 162). Furthermore, Labour's 2015 electoral loss resulted from "Ed Miliband's failure, at least as the Labour left saw it, to mount a full-blooded assault on austerity"(Bale 2015: 18). Early research on the political profile of

Corbyn supporters found that they "overwhelmingly describe themselves as left-wing. They reject capitalism … and favour higher taxes to pay for greater welfare."[1] Ideologically, the rise of the SNP, the Green Surge and the election of Jeremy Corbyn contain a common thread of revolt against the establishment Left's erstwhile accommodating, or even facilitating, approach to fiscal austerity.

A divide between moderates, on the one hand, who, in the name of electability, had previously dominated centre-left party machines and, on the other, radicals who decry the former's apologetic approach to austerity, is hardly a unique experience to Britain. A number of centre-left parties in Western democracies have either gone into decline at the expense of radical newcomers—such as Greece's PASOK, Spain's PSOE, Portugal's Socialist Party and Ireland's Labour Party—or have seen new members rally around a radical outsider within the party—such as the Democratic Party in the USA. The former cases can largely be explained by the austerity regimes imposed after 2010, however, in the USA there was no such fiscal austerity programme. Instead, Bernie Sanders, a leftist Democratic presidential candidate, has risen to prominence in protest against the power of the financial services industry and by arguing for a larger state, protectionist trade policies, removal of university tuition fees, a higher minimum wage, higher taxes, an amnesty for illegal immigrants, universal health care and a large scale fiscal stimulus based on the creation of green jobs and infrastructure. The similarity between the policies of Bernie Sanders and those of the Greens in Britain suggests the possibility of a common explanation for the growth of both. In this sense, the rallying cry of 'anti-austerity' by the SNP, the Greens and Corbyn in Britain and elsewhere was less of a contribution to the debate on the merits of a Keynesian fiscal responses to economic downturns and more of a denouncement of a broader economic system by segments of the electorate on either side of the Atlantic who blame 'neo-liberalism' for the economic crisis and widening inequality.

There has also been growth in support for a number of Green parties across Europe since 2008, particularly in countries in which those parties had traditionally been weak. Green parties in France, Norway, Sweden, Denmark, Iceland, Hungary, Latvia and Croatia have all seen their electoral results improve since the financial crisis, although often from very low, or non-existent, baselines. In Greece and Spain, Green parties have aligned themselves with the populist left Syriza and Podemos, respectively, securing small parliamentary representation and, in the former case, a position in government. In the 2016 German regional election, the Greens finished first in the Baden-Württemberg state election though their vote share dropped in the two other concurrent regional elections. In the 2016 Austrian Presidential election, a Green candidate defeated the populist right Freedom Party in an extremely close election. Future research should investigate the causes of the relative growth in Green support across southern, eastern and non-Eurozone northern Europe. By contrast, Green parties in Canada, Australia and New Zealand have seen their impressive growth throughout the 2000s either stop or even reverse since 2010.

Where do Britain's Greens parties go from here? In the 2016 Scottish Parliament elections, the Greens increased their parliamentary representation from two to six seats. As before, Greens were elected entirely via Holyrood's proportional regional list election, in which they finished ahead of the Liberal Democrats, rather than the simultaneous first-past-the-post constituency election. Their popular Co-Convenor, Patrick Harvie, continuously campaigned on the idea that the Scottish Greens would "push the SNP beyond their comfort zone."[2] Harvie's party used leaders' debates to argue, first, in favour of higher taxes for the rich in order to avoid public spending cuts and, second, for environmentalist positions on issues such as energy efficiency, emissions and fracking. With the Scottish party system now divided by a nationalist-unionist axis, as well as the traditional left-right axis, the Scottish Greens' greater relevance and success seems secure for now.

The fate of the Green Party of England and Wales is less clear. The Labour Party was already the main threat to the Greens, so, with the election of a radical leftist leader, the GPEW risks sudden irrelevance, despite the immense progress it has made in recent years. Party insiders are mixed in their estimations of how Corbyn will affect their party. Caroline Lucas is typically professional, stating "We welcome the opportunity to work with him, we're very glad that now there's somebody alongside us who is saying some of the same things that we've been saying for years." Others are quicker to clarify the threat that a Corbyn-led Labour Party represents to the GPEW. Dee Searle, 2015 candidate for Tottenham, states, "I think in the past we were slightly there by default because people were so frustrated with Labour. What it means to us now is that we've really got to sort our politics out." Darren Hall, 2015 candidate in Bristol West, takes a broader view, "If we continue to professionalise and respond to some of these massive global issues that are starting to emerge ... refugees, global warming, some stuff that's bound to happen ... then we genuinely could become the third biggest party in the UK ... if we end up hitching our wagon to Corbyn too closely, I think we could go down with that ship."

Key for the GPEW will be maintaining members and, thus, resources. The party's increase in vote share in 2015 was partially the result of its new ability to stand candidates in far more seats than before. It is unlikely that the party will see another 'Green Surge', not least because that phenomenon was underpinned by enthusiastic journalists who were eager to 'discover' the party and speculate, for some time, on its potential to 'shake up' British politics. The Green Surge was also, more fundamentally, the result of a distinct ideological group who felt unrepresented by any other political party during a Parliament dominated by public spending cuts and anti-immigration rhetoric. Highly public internal division within the Labour Party, of which there are already clear signs, will likely assist the Greens in those seats where Labour's MP or candidate is an outspoken opponent of Jeremy Corbyn. Moreover, Greens would be wise to remember that over half of their 2015 voters were previously Liberal Democrat voters. The demise of the Liberal Democrats looks to be relatively enduring and it remains to be seen whether Labour will be able to increase their success in many of the Liberal Democrat's previous heartlands. The GPEW will continue to perform relatively well in the handful of constituencies in which there is no other opposition to the Conservatives or Labour, not least because the local Green parties are often far more established in such seats. The party finished third in both the 2016 London Mayoral and Assembly elections, though, in the concurrent English local elections, the party's performances were mixed and saw them lose three seats, which was widely interpreted by the media as the result of Corbyn's leadership of the Labour Party.

As voters have become more willing to switch between parties, British politics has become less predictable. As Natalie Bennett says, "politics is incredibly uncertain. The one certainty is change; the future of politics doesn't look like the past ... If we got electoral reform, that would be utterly transformative ... There is no guarantee in 20 years' time that we'll have a British politics in which you have a dominant Labour Party and a dominant Tory Party." For now, with a distinct target demographic, large membership, 'professionalised' structure and considerably greater representation than just a few years earlier, the Greens are an accepted member of the second tier of Britain's refigured party system and better placed to make a meaningful impact on British politics than ever before.

Notes

1. Kellner, P. (2015), 'New polling data shows the challenge facing Jeremy Corbyn', accessed at http://www.newstatesman.com/politics/uk/2015/09/new-polling-data-shows-challenge-facing-jeremy-corbyn on 03/05/2016.
2. Brooks, L. (2016), 'Patrick Harvie: Scottish Greens will push SNP beyond their comfort zone', accessed at http://www.theguardian.com/uk-news/scotland-blog/2016/may/04/patrick-harvie-scottish-greens-will-push-the-snp-beyond-their-comfort-zone on 4/5/2016.

Bibliography

Bale, T. (2015), 'The Loser Takes It All. Labour and Jeremy Corbyn. A Response to Steve Richards' in *The Political Quarterly*, 87 (1), 18–19

Clarke, H., Kellner, P., Stewart, M. C., Twyman, J. and Whiteley, P. (2016), *Austerity and Political Choice in Britain*, Basingstoke: Palgrave

Mitchell, J. (2015), 'Sea Change in Scotland' in *Parliamentary Affairs*, 68 (suppl 1), 88–100

Bibliography

Bornschier, S. and Kriesi, H. (2013), 'The populist right, the working class, and the changing face of class politics' in ed. Rydgren, J. *Class Politics and the Radical Right.* Oxford: Routledge, 10–30

Burnside, R., Herbert, S. and Curtis, S. (2003), 'Election 2003', *SPICe briefing,* Scottish Parliament

Curtice, J. (1989), 'The 1989 European Election: Protest or Green Tide?' in *Electoral Studies*, 8, 217–230.

Dommett, K. (2013), 'A Miserable Little Compromise? Exploring Liberal Democrat Fortunes in the UK Coalition' in *The Political Quarterly*, 84 (2), 218–227

Downs, A. (1957), *An Economic Theory of Democracy*, New York: Harper

Ford, R. and Goodwin, M. (2014), 'Understanding UKIP: Identity, Social Change and the Left Behind' in *The Political Quarterly*, 85 (3), 274–287

Kitschelt, H. (1994), The Transformation of European Social Democracy, Cambridge: Cambridge University Press, p. 227

Lowe P. and Rudig, W. (1986), 'Political Ecology and the Social Sciences: The State of the Art' in *British Journal of Political Science*, 16, 513–550.

Richardson, R. and Rootes, C. (eds.) (1996), *The Green Challenge: The Development of Green Parties in Europe*, London: Routledge

J. Dennison, *The Greens in British Politics*,
DOI 10.1007/978-3-319-42673-0

Index

A
amateur-activists, 42–9
anti-capitalism, 15, 16, 18
anti-establishment sentiment, 28
austerity, 1, 7, 11, 16–19, 21–4, 36, 41, 55, 63, 73, 88, 96, 97, 100, 112, 113, 120, 135–8, 141, 142

B
Bennett, Natalie
  interviews, 88, 90, 94
    consequences, 2, 109
  leader ratings, 4, 15, 17, 38, 51 59n6, 65, 83–91, 94, 110, 118, 136
  party management, 93, 110
Blair, Tony, 25, 31n23, 31n25, 76, 99
Blue Labour, 23
Brighton Pavilion, 3, 43, 78, 98, 99, 108, 131n1
Bristol West, 15, 17, 27, 46, 78, 99–101, 108, 129, 131n1, 143
British Election Study, 8, 17, 18, 20, 21, 40, 54, 90, 98, 103, 104n16, 108

C
Cameron, David, 25, 26, 31n20, 31n25, 64, 65, 67, 68, 72, 80n1, 81n16, 88, 90
Chapel Hill Expert Survey, 8, 9n7, 15
Clegg, Nick, 18–21, 30n11, 30n13, 72, 88, 90, 129
Coalition Agreement, 18, 19, 21
coalition government, 11, 16, 18, 138
communications, 7, 43–5, 48, 63, 66, 85, 100
Conservative party, 66, 77
Constituency effects, 123
constitutional amendment, 16, 17
Corbyn, Jeremy, 135, 141–4, 145n1
crowdfunding, 129

E
environmentalism, 11, 37, 50, 55, 57, 74, 95, 105n24, 107, 109, 115, 120, 136–8, 140
European Green Party Membership Survey (EGPM), 69

J. Dennison, *The Greens in British Politics*,
DOI 10.1007/978-3-319-42673-0

F
Farage, Nigel, 14, 26–8, 29n3, 31n28, 32n33, 64, 66, 67, 73, 88, 90
first-past-the-post electoral system, 3, 75, 83
Fixed Term Parliaments Act (2011), 64
focus groups, 15, 97
fundraising
  donations, 44, 45, 77

G
gender, 26, 65, 68, 70, 76, 110
globalism, 17, 20, 24
GPEx. *See* Green Party Executive Committee (GPEx)
Green Party Executive Committee (GPEx), 13, 43, 45, 46, 48, 68, 77, 78, 89, 92, 93
Green Party in Northern Ireland, 1, 2, 8
Green Party of England and Wales
  credibility, 85, 86, 92, 94, 136
  polling, 4, 35, 68, 84
Green Surge
  increased resources, 77–80
  increase in capability, 44
  new members, 4, 67, 68, 72, 101, 138, 142

H
Harvie, Patrick, 51, 52, 55, 57, 61n30, 143, 145n2

I
immigration, 7, 11, 23–7, 29, 36, 37, 55, 64, 73, 84, 87, 88, 92, 94, 95, 97, 98, 105n24, 112, 120, 135, 139, 141
integration-demarcation, 26, 110, 138

L
Labour Party, 7, 11, 17, 21–4, 49, 50, 66, 72, 75–7, 99, 101, 135, 138, 142–4
leader ratings, 4, 9, 11, 52, 65, 83, 84
left-libertarian, 12, 20, 21, 35, 49, 88, 109, 126, 131, 138, 141
Liberal Democrats, 4, 8, 11, 14, 18–22, 25, 26, 29, 38, 40, 42, 64, 66, 69, 72, 76, 99, 103, 107, 112, 113, 116, 118, 120, 124, 125, 129–31, 135–8, 140, 141, 143, 144
Lucas, Caroline, 15, 16, 24, 28, 36, 43, 45, 65, 77, 78, 80n7, 86, 94–9, 104n10, 143

M
media coverage, 27, 35, 37, 40, 64, 66, 67, 137
Miliband, Ed, 8, 11, 21–4, 26, 28, 30n11, 30n17, 31n18, 31n19, 31n22, 31n28, 59n10, 66, 72, 81n14, 88, 90, 120, 138, 141
multiculturalism, 23, 25

N
New Labour, 22–4, 66, 138
1989 European Parliament elections, 12
Norwich South, 20, 99, 100, 130, 131n1

O
organisational change
  centralisation, 42
  internal democracy, 48
  professionalisation, 42, 43, 45, 46, 48
  resistance, 48

P
party membership, decline in UK, 2, 6
Party Members Project (PMP), 8, 68, 69, 71, 72, 74
party system change, 1, 2, 132n2, 136
Plaid Cymru, 68, 87, 126
Podemos, 28, 139, 142
Policies for a Sustainable Society (PSS), 92
populism, 11, 28
post-materialism, 109
professional-electoralists, 42, 47
public spending cuts, 16–18, 73, 112, 137, 143, 144

S
Scottish Greens
  membership surge, 3, 52, 53, 58
Scottish Independence Referendum
  Green Yes, 51
  Radical Independence Campaign (RIC), 51
  Yes Scotland, 50, 51, 58
Scottish National Party (SNP), 35, 49–55, 57, 58, 68, 69, 87, 108, 111–13, 139–43
Scottish Socialist Party (SSP), 49, 50, 53
SNP. *See* Scottish National Party (SNP)
SSP. *See* Scottish Socialist Party (SSP)
Syriza, 28, 139, 142

T
target-to-win, 46, 47, 49, 129
televised leaders debates
  Ofcom, 66–8
  petition, 7
  public attitudes, 63
tuition fees, 19, 22, 37, 95, 142
2014 European Parliament elections
  Green campaigning, 36, 49, 50, 55, 58, 78, 143
  Green manifesto, 27, 78
  polling spike, 40
  spill-over, 35
2014 local elections, 40
2015 general election
  constituency campaigning, 7, 45, 98–103, 131
  Green campaigning, 21, 83
    party political broadcast, 13
  Green manifesto, 26
    launch, 94–6
    Manifesto Working Group, 93, 94
  Green voters, 21, 38, 108
2015 Labour Party leadership election, 141
2015 local election, 8, 12, 36, 144
2016 Scottish Parliament elections, 143

U
UK Independence Party (UKIP), 3, 4, 8, 11, 14, 23, 25–9, 35, 37, 47, 63–7, 69, 73, 76, 78, 88, 91, 96–8, 110, 113, 118, 127, 135–9
UKIP. *See* UK Independence Party (UKIP)
UKIP of the left, 3, 64, 91, 135, 138, 139

Printed by Printforce, the Netherlands